AA

North
York Moors

C. Fallis & J FALLIS
12094 216 St.
Maple Ridge, BC V2X 5J3

2004

AA Publishing

Author: John Morrison

Page layout: Jo Tapper

Produced by AA Publishing
© Automobile Association
Developments Ltd 1996, 1999,
2002.

Published by AA Publishing
(a trading name of Automobile
Association Developments Limited,
whose registered office is
Millstream, Maidenhead Road,
Windsor, Berkshire, SL4 5GD.
Registered Number 1878835)

First edition published 1996,
reprinted 1996, 1997, 1998.
Second edition 1999,
reprinted 2000.
Third edition 2002.

Ordnance Survey® This product
includes
mapping data licensed from
Ordnance Survey® with the
permission of the Controller of Her
Majesty's Stationery Office.
© Crown copyright 2002. All rights
reserved. Licence number 399221.

Mapping produced by the
Cartographic Department of The
Automobile Association. A00691.

ISBN 07495 3296 3

A CIP catalogue record for this
book is available from the British
Library.

Gazetteer map references are taken
from the National Grid and can be
used in conjunction with Ordnance
Survey maps and atlases. Places
featured in this guide will not
necessarily be found on the maps
at the back of the book.

All the walks are on rights of way,
permissive paths or on routes
where de facto access for walkers
is accepted. On routes which are
not on legal rights of way, but
where access for walkers is allowed
by local agreements, no
implication of a right of way is
intended.

The contents of this book are
believed correct at the time of
printing. Nevertheless, the
publishers cannot accept
responsibility for errors or
omissions, or for changes in
details given in this guide or for
the consequences of any reliance
on the information it provides. We
have tried to ensure accuracy in
this book, but things do change
and we would be grateful if
readers would advise us of any
inaccuracies they may encounter.

Visit the AA Publishing website at
www.theAA.com

Colour reproduction by L C Repro

Printed and bound by G. Canale &
C. S.P.A., Torino, Italy.

Contents

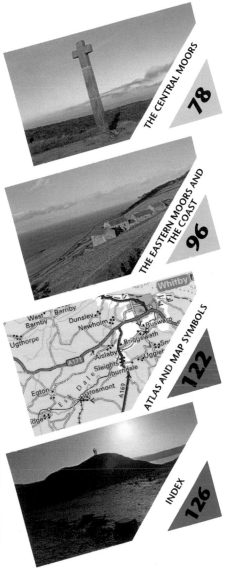

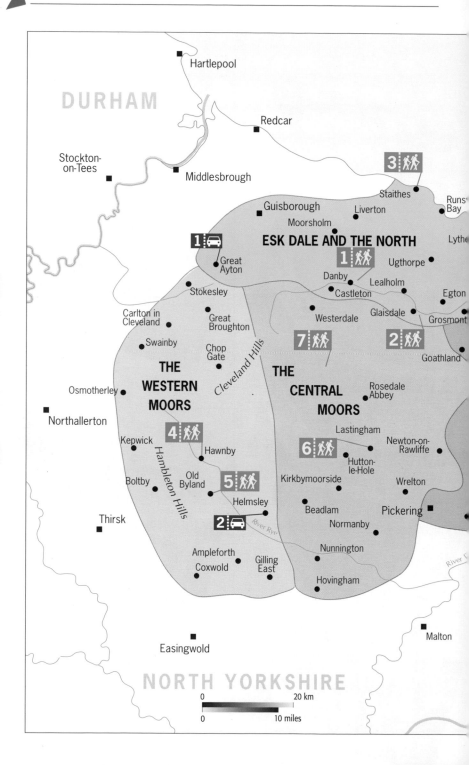

Hartlepool

DURHAM

Redcar

Stockton-on-Tees

Middlesbrough

3 🥾🥾

Staithes

Runs Bay

Guisborough

Liverton

Moorsholm

Lythe

1 🚗

ESK DALE AND THE NORTH

Great Ayton

1 🥾🥾

Ugthorpe

Danby

Lealholm

Egton

Stokesley

Castleton

Carlton in Cleveland

Great Broughton

Westerdale

Glaisdale

Grosmont

Swainby

7 🥾🥾

2 🥾🥾

Chop Gate

Cleveland Hills

Goathland

THE WESTERN MOORS

THE CENTRAL MOORS

Rosedale Abbey

Osmotherley

Northallerton

Lastingham

Newton-on-Rawcliffe

Kepwick

4 🥾🥾

6 🥾🥾

Hawnby

Hutton-le-Hole

Boltby

Old Byland

5 🥾🥾

Kirkbymoorside

Wrelton

Hambleton Hills

Helmsley

Pickering

2 🚗

River Rye

Beadlam

Thirsk

Normanby

Ampleforth

Nunnington

River

Coxwold

Gilling East

Hovingham

Easingwold

Malton

NORTH YORKSHIRE

0   20 km

0   10 miles

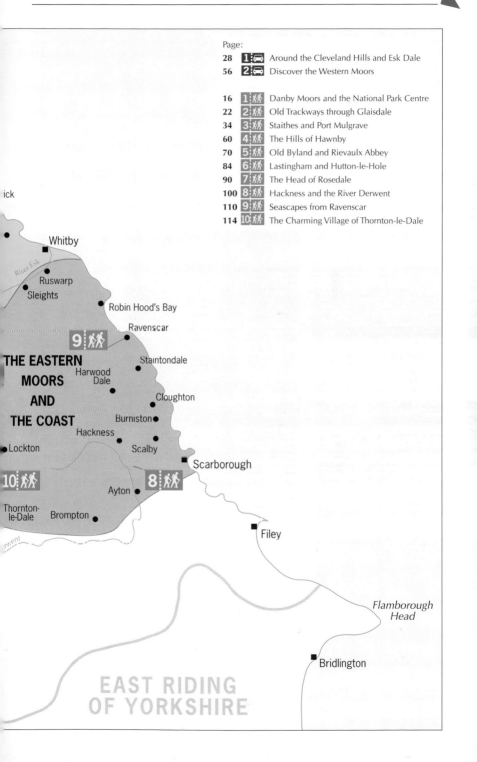

ick

Whitby

River Esk

Ruswarp

Sleights

Robin Hood's Bay

Ravenscar

9 🚶

THE EASTERN

Staintondale

MOORS

Harwood
Dale

AND

Cloughton

THE COAST

Burniston

Hackness

Lockton

Scalby

Scarborough

10 🚶

8 🚶

Ayton

Thornton-
le-Dale

Brompton

Filey

Derwent

*Flamborough
Head*

Bridlington

EAST RIDING
OF YORKSHIRE

Introducing The North York Moors

At one time the North York Moors were known as 'Blackamore', and had a reputation for being bleak and awe-inspiring, even frightening. But the visitors of today have a very different view of the moors and dales, coming here to enjoy the 'quiet recreational' that underpins the National Park philosophy.

There is much to enjoy – the largest acreage of heather moorland in the country, spectacular coastal scenery and a clutch of compact villages still unspoiled by the worst excesses of the tourist trade. It's an expansive landscape, with room to roam. The moors, carpeted with purple heather in late summer, are a wonderful place to fill the lungs with unpolluted air, heave a rucksack over the shoulder and strike out towards some distant landmark. ◆

WAYMARKERS
Scores of standing stones scattered across the North York Moors indicate ancient boundaries and byways, marking out the past, right

DELIGHTFUL VILLAGES
There are dozens of pretty villages to explore, including Egton Bridge, left, in the valley of the River Esk

QUEEN OF RESORTS
The rugged North Yorkshire coastline offers outstanding fishing bays and holiday centres, including Scarborough, above, queen of them all

THE CLEVELAND WAY
For serious walkers, several famous long-distance footpaths cross the region, including the Cleveland Way, below

NATIONAL PARK
Above, the North York Moors National Park was created in 1952; its functions are revealed at the visitor centre in Danby

THE 'MOUSEMAN'
A craftsman carves a wooden mouse in Robert Thompson's workshop in Kilburn, thus continuing the tradition of the celebrated 'Mouseman'

GREAT AYTON
Left, the village of Great Ayton has become a popular centre in the region thanks to the exploits of Captain James Cook who attended the local school

CAPTAIN JAMES COOK
Above, the navigator Captain Cook is commemorated in a number of locations, linked today by the Cook Heritage Trail

TEN BEST CHURCHES AND ABBEYS

Rievaulx Abbey
Mount Grace Priory, nr Osmotherley
St Mary's Church and Crypt, Lastingham
St Gregory's Minster, Kirkdale
St Mary's Church and Abbey, Whitby
Byland Abbey
Church of St Peter and St Paul, Pickering
St Peter's Church, Hackness
St Hilda's Church, Ellerburn
Church of All Saints, Great Ayton

CHURCH OF ST HILDA
Right, the mellow old church at Ellerburn, near Pickering, rewards a closer look

A GOLDEN DALE
Springtime brings a spectacular display of golden, dancing daffodils at Farndale, left

MOORLAND GRAZING
Right, the ubiquitous moorland sheep are a reminder that this is a landscape shaped by farming as well as industry over the centuries

THE ESSENTIAL NORTH YORK MOORS

If you have little time and you want to sample the essence of the North York Moors:

Enjoy the view across the Vale of York from the top of Sutton Bank... **Walk** part (or all!) of the Cleveland Way, which starts at Helmsley and ends at Filey Brigg on the coast... **Visit** Staithes, a perfect Yorkshire fishing village... **Hunt** for Whitby jet in the town's antiques shops, or watch it being made in the craftsmens' workshops... **Steam** along the North Yorkshire Moors Railway, which runs from Pickering to Grosmont... **Search** for a small carved mouse, Robert Thompson's unique trademark, on the furniture in local churches, and then visit the workshops at Kilburn... **Linger** by the extensive remains of Rievaulx Abbey... **Admire** the daffodils of Farndale... **Look out** for the moorland crosses, there are more than a thousand of them on the moors... **Follow in the steps** of Roman soldiers and walk along Wade's Causeway... **Take** the scenic Newtondale Forest Drive through Cropton Forest.

A Weekend in the North York Moors: Day One

For many people a weekend break or a long weekend is a popular way of spending their leisure time.

These four pages offer a loosely planned itinerary designed to ensure that you make the most of your time, whatever the weather, and see and enjoy the very best the area has to offer. Places with gazetteer entries are in **bold**.

Friday Night

Stay at the Feversham Arms in **Helmsley**. This charming hotel, just a few yards from the Market Square, has its own swimming pool and offers a touch of luxury with four-poster beds in many of the rooms. The restaurant is renowned for its good food (especially shellfish and game in season) and outstanding wine list.

Left, in Helmsley look out for the ancient castle

Below, marvel at the skills of the builders of Rievaulx Abbey

Saturday Morning

Your first stop should be the Tourist Information Centre in the Market Square for details of any events that may be happening at the weekend. A short drive from Helmsley, on the B1257, is **Rievaulx Abbey**, one of Yorkshire's architectural gems, in a splendid setting in the valley of the River Rye.

Minor roads (have a road map to hand) lead southwest to the village of **Kilburn**. Beneath the distinctive hill figure of the White Horse is the showroom of Robert Thompson's

Craftsmen, who keep alive the tradition and artistry of the world famous 'Mouseman'. Opposite the showroom is the visitor centre.

Saturday Lunch

Drive the short distance east to **Byland Abbey** where, directly opposite the ruins, you'll find the Abbey Inn. The stone-flagged floor, antique furniture and imaginative menu make this the ideal place for lunch.

Don't miss the modern craft skills displayed at Kilburn, above

Survey the moors in vintage style on the train from Pickering, right

Take a walk in the dramatic landscape of the Hole of Horcum, below

Saturday Afternoon

Pass Helmsley once again and continue east along the A170 to **Pickering**, the terminus of the **North Yorkshire Moors Railway**. This preserved line offers a nostalgic return to the age of steam. A round trip to **Goathland** will show you some of the finest scenery in the National Park, as well as giving you time to explore the moorland village now best known as a location for the popular television series *Heartbeat*.

On your return to Pickering, drive north up the A169, passing the huge natural amphitheatre known as the **Hole of Horcum**, towards the port of **Whitby**.

Saturday Night

Three miles (4.8km) north of the bustling town, signed off the A171, is Dunsley Hall Hotel, an impressive Victorian mansion in the quiet village of Dunsley where you can escape from the crowds.

A Weekend in the North York Moors: Day Two

Our second and final day starts with a visit to the bustling resort of Whitby and a nearby picturesque fishing village, before driving along the beautiful Esk Valley and across the moors, passing through a number of lovely villages, before arriving back in Helmsley.

Sunday Morning

Explore **Whitby** on foot. It's a fascinating town, with surprises at every turn in its winding streets. The abbey, St Mary's Church, the Captain Cook Museum and the harbour are just a few of the 'musts'.

On a different scale are the tiny fishing villages of **Staithes** (north of Whitby) and **Robin Hood's Bay** (a few miles to the south). Both are achingly picturesque; take time to explore one or the other.

Afterwards, a leisurely drive along the beautiful Esk Valley, passing the villages of **Grosmont, Glaisdale** (look out for the Beggar's Bridge) and **Lealholm** will bring you to **Danby**. At the Moors Centre you can learn how the moorland landscape came to look the way it does, and perhaps have coffee.

Drive south from Danby, along Blakey Ridge (an unclassified road, more map reading needed). With the valley of **Rosedale** to your left and **Farndale** to your right, this is moorland scenery at its best.

Enjoy the winding streets of old Whitby, above

Take a stroll through the narrow alleyways of Robin Hood's Bay, left

Sunday Lunch

Look out for the Lion Inn, miles from anywhere on Blakey Ridge, where travellers have long received a warm welcome. Our suggested itinerary should make this a late lunch. No problem, the Lion Inn serves its excellent meals throughout the day.

Drive along Blakey Ridge for the best dales views, above

Admire the showpiece village of Hutton le Hole, right

Wild flowers flourish in the churchyard at Lastingham, below

Sunday Afternoon

Continue driving along Blakey Ridge, with perhaps a moorland walk to fill the lungs with pure upland air. Look out for the guide stones on the roadside (see page 93). The road brings you to **Hutton-le-Hole**, one of Yorkshire's picture-postcard villages and well worth exploring. Near by is **Lastingham**; our Walk on page 84 offers an excellent way to see both villages.

Our weekend started with one monastic gem and ends with another intriguing religious site. The church at Lastingham has a 'secret' crypt, built almost a thousand years ago.

Drive west along the A170 to arrive back in Helmsley where you can enjoy afternoon tea before heading for home.

Esk Dale and the North

The River Esk meanders enticingly from its source on the moors near Westerdale, linking a number of lovely villages before reaching the North Sea with a flourish – dividing the fascinating fishing port of Whitby into two. From source to sea the Esk is a delight; the valley road between Stokesley and Whitby crosses and recrosses it many times. Rail travellers follow the course of the Esk more closely on the scenic line between Middlesbrough and Whitby. But the best way to see Esk Dale is on foot. The Esk Valley Walk, a waymarked route, begins at Castleton and follows the river, and the villages along its banks, to the coast at Whitby.

MOORLAND 'INTAKES'
It's a sudden contrast where the fields stop and open moorland begins, showing that the fields higher up the valley sides are 'intakes': that is, land 'taken in' from the moorland above. At the head of many moorland valleys are ruined farmsteads, abandoned when the living became too precarious. Here you often see unmanaged grassy pasture inexorably reverting back to heather and bracken.

CASTLETON   Map ref NZ6807
The castle is long gone from Castleton, only the name and a tell-tale mound to the north of the village remain – unsentimentally, a lot of the stone from the castle may have been recycled in the building of Danby Castle. Castleton used to have regular markets and a goods yard on the railway; the markets have gone, but the village still has its passenger station on the Esk Valley railway line.

The River Esk, which rises at Esklets in Westerdale to the south, is joined by a tributary, Commondale Beck, at Castleton. To the north of the village is an expanse of moorland, but the landscape is very different from that

A pair of cosy cottages at Castleton

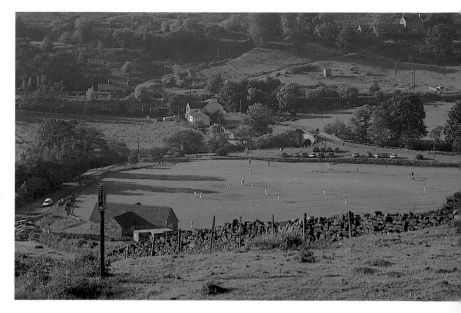

Castleton's cricket pitch is beautifully set on the valley bottom

of the south, with a selection of minor roads, tracks and good footpaths exploring a landscape of great variety. Two routes 'take the high road' over Castleton Rigg, enjoying panoramic views down into Westerdale and Danby Dale, and on to Ralph Cross (the template for the National Park emblem) and the head of beautiful Rosedale. This is moorland scenery at its best; valley bottoms divided up into neat fields by drystone walls, the pattern interrupted by little copses.

You would hesitate to call Commondale, northwest on the Esk Valley line, one of the prettier villages on the moors. This scattering of houses and farms occupies a hillside overlooking Commondale Moor. The village's most striking aspect is the use of brick, as much as stone, as a building material – the diminutive brick-built Church of St Peter, in particular, stands out like the proverbial sore thumb. The reason is simple: until the 1950s Commondale had its own brickworks, and bricks and tiles form decorative elements in a number of houses throughout the village, and on the façade of the old Co-op shop.

The village name was once written as 'Colmandale'. It is said that Colman, Bishop of Lindisfarne, stopped off here on his travels to Whitby Abbey.

DANBY   Map ref NZ7008

The village of Danby lies on a crossroads; blink and you've missed it. But it was to this little village that John Atkinson came, at the age of 36, as minister of the parish. He was Essex-born and until the end of his long life retained the natural curiosity of the newcomer. One

A TIRELESS MAN
Canon J C Atkinson, minister of Danby parish church in the 19th century, took three wives, fathered 13 children and still found time to indulge in a number of social and intellectual pursuits. He consigned his fascinating observations and opinions to a diary, later published as *Forty Years in a Moorland Parish*.

The graceful curve of Duck Bridge spans the River Esk

DUCK BRIDGE

Duck Bridge, a superb late 14th-century example of an arched packhorse bridge, is a tangible reminder of a time when sturdy ponies, laden down with twin pannier bags, were the principal means by which goods were transported from town to town. The name has two possible origins: either honouring a benefactor, George Duck, said to have paid for its repair, or a corruption of 'Duke's Bridge'.

CYCLING IN THE ESK VALLEY

The minor roads between Castleton, Danby and Lealholm in the Esk Valley are ideal for cycling as they are quiet and the valley floor level. With a little help from the OS Landranger map Sheet 94 1:50,000 it is possible to avoid most of the steep gradients on the roads out of the valley.

of his major passions was prehistory, and the moors – with their burial mounds, standing stones and wayside crosses – provided much to excite his inquiring mind. He died in 1900, and is buried in the churchyard.

There are a number of interesting features in the immediate vicinity, and the easiest way to see them is to park at the National Park's Visitor Centre, just half a mile (800m) from the village on the road to Lealholm. The Moors Centre represents the public face of the National Park. Here visitors can discover what makes the North York Moors so special.

The building which houses the Moors Centre was once a shooting lodge for the Dawnay family, who bought the Manor of Danby as far back as 1656; it now hosts exhibitions and a wide variety of events, including guided walks. The evolution of the moorland landscape is fully explained, and those whose needs extend no further than a mug of tea are equally well catered for.

The Moors Centre sits in 13 acres (5.2ha) of land, close to the Esk, a lovely spot to enjoy a picnic or a riverside stroll. A number of waymarked walks explore the immediate environs; longer walks (such as the one on page 16) take the car park as their starting point.

A few yards downstream is a fine arched packhorse bridge, intriguingly named Duck Bridge. The packhorse trail leads towards Danby Castle, once a fortified house of some distinction, though most of the medieval stonework has since been incorporated into a farmhouse; there is only limited public access. The castle, built in the 14th century, was once the home of Catherine Parr, the sixth wife of Henry VIII, who fared better than his other wives and, indeed, survived him. Past Danby Castle Farm the road explores a minor valley; Little Fryup Dale is as delightful as it sounds.

EGTON BRIDGE   Map ref NZ8004

Egton and Egton Bridge are a pair of villages separated by both the River Esk and a steep descent. Egton has nothing to do with eggs; it appeared in the Domesday Book as Egetune, meaning 'the town of the oak trees'. The oaks are long gone, as are the annual hiring fairs, when farmers would look to employ farm labourers for the forthcoming year. Even the weekly markets, for which the village was granted a charter by William of Orange, are no longer held in the village's broad street. But the village is the venue, every August, for one of the area's largest horse and agricultural shows.

A new bridge, built in 1993, spans the Esk at Egton Bridge. The stone arch replaces an ugly metal structure that was itself merely a replacement for the original bridge, which was swept away in floods in the 1930s.

Egton Bridge was the birthplace in 1599 of Father Nicholas Postgate, who ministered to his Catholic flock at much danger to himself. For the 'crime' of baptising a child into the Catholic faith, Father Postgate was sent for trial at York. In 1678 he was subjected – he was in his 80s – to the ultimate punishment, being hanged, drawn and quartered. In remaining staunchly Roman Catholic, Egton Bridge became known as 'the village missed by the Reformation'. The impressive Catholic Church of St Hedda contains relics of Father Postgate's ministry. Half-way up the hill to Egton is a house with a tiny chapel hidden in the roof, reached by a secret passage. The hidden room was only rediscovered 150 years after Postgate's death, since when the house has been known as the Mass House.

Every year, in August, the famous Egton Bridge Gooseberry Show is held. You will have to be a spectator rather than a competitor – at least until you are voted in as a member of the Old Gooseberry Society, founded in 1800. Size, not taste, is what matters here.

Ramblers alight at Egton Bridge, a stop on the Middlesbrough to Whitby line, and walk along the Esk Valley to Lealholm to catch the next train home.

EGTON'S BARGUEST

Egton was once believed to have its own barguest, or spectral hound. Such beasts, with their blazing eyes the size of saucers, feature regularly in northern folklore. To see a barguest was an ill omen, presaging a death or other tragedy. A barguest made occasional appearances between Egton and Egton Bridge, its fearsome howls driving icy terror into all who had the misfortune to come across it.

A tranquil corner at Egton Bridge

Danby Moors and the National Park Centre

A ramble across the moors overlooking Esk Dale, with gorgeous views down into Little Fryup Dale. The walk starts and finishes at the Moors Centre, the National Park's visitor centre near Danby.

Time: 2½ hours. Distance: 4½ miles (7.2km).
Location: 7½ miles (12.1km) southeast of Guisborough.
Start: Park at the Moors Centre, a mile (1.6km) east of Danby village on the road to Lealholm. (OS grid ref: NZ717084.)
OS Map: Outdoor Leisure 27 (North York Moors – Eastern area) 1:25,000.
See Key to Walks on page 123.

ROUTE DIRECTIONS

From the car park, cross the road and instead of walking up to the **Moors Centre** itself, take the path to the left, waymarked 'Danby Village'. Cross the River Esk on a footbridge and follow the fence at the field edge to the railway line: cross the line with care. Follow a green broad track to a stile and turn right along a very minor road. Pass some fairly new houses and, as the road bears left, take the path between stone posts and continue downhill to rejoin the road. Turn right, recrossing both the River Esk and the railway line and pass

Esk Mill (known locally as Danby Watermill), and continue up into the village of **Danby**.

Turn right before the public house; beyond the houses follow the bridleway sign to the left. The track zigzags up the hill, continues through gorse alongside a wall, and goes uphill to a pair of gates. Go through the right-hand gate and continue uphill to meet the end of a wall and a choice of tracks. Take the grassy track to the left, Lord's Turnpike, which offers easy walking across unenclosed moorland, down to a road. Turn right, ignoring the first footpath sign, and take a bridleway to the right, signposted to 'Clither Beck Farm'.

When the track forks right into the farmyard, keep straight ahead; soon you get delightful views down into

The National Park visitor centre near Danby was formerly a shooting lodge

Clither Beck Valley. The track follows a fence, crosses a beck then bears right. When the fence turns abruptly to the right, take the left-hand track and continue ahead, passing old mine workings. Follow the track to a T-junction of minor roads. Keep straight ahead, along an unenclosed road and shortly cross another road to walk downhill, through Oakley Side, on a broad track between walls. Enjoy the splendid views ahead of Little Fryup Dale and Ainthorpe Rigg, the hill to the right.

Meet another minor road and turn right, downhill. In a short distance, when the road turns sharp left, continue straight ahead on a track leading through a farmyard. When the track goes left down to another farm, cross a stile ahead waymarked 'Esk Valley Way'. Follow the field edge to another stile, walk through the middle of the next field to a stile and out on to the road. Turn right and return to the Moors Centre and your car.

POINTS OF INTEREST

The Moors Centre

Danby Lodge, set in its own parkland on the banks of the River Esk, was built as a shooting lodge for the members of the Dawnay family, who have enjoyed power and influence in these parts for centuries. Since 1975 the lodge has served as the main visitor centre for the North York Moors National Park, and is open every day from Easter to October, and at weekends during the rest of the year. The varied programme features exhibitions, talks, walks and other activities, offering something for all tastes and ages. The Living Landscape, one of the exhibitions, details the evolution of these moors and dales.

Esk Mill

The waters of the River Esk used to turn the wheels of a number of mills, but Esk Mill, more than 350 years old, is the only one still in working order, though it is not open to the public.

Danby

Danby's main claim to fame is that its castle (the remains are incorporated into a farmhouse and are not open to the public) was once owned by Catherine Parr, the sixth wife of Henry VIII, and the only one to survive him. Otherwise this is a typical Moors village with a traditional welcoming pub, The Duke of Wellington, situated at the crossroads. For more information on Danby see the entry on page 13.

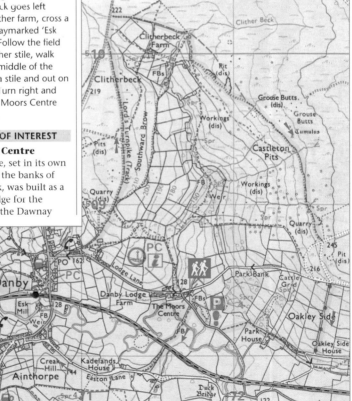

AN OLD BALLAD

AN OLD BALLAD

When Tom Ferris built Beggar's Bridge across the Esk the occasion was marked by an old ballad, of which one of the verses runs:

'The Rover came back from a far distant land
And claimed of the maiden her long promised hand,
But he built 'ere he won her the bridge of his vow
And lovers from Egton pass over it now.'

Tom's initials and the date, 1619, are still visible on the eastern capstone of the bridge.

The rolling hills of Glaisdale are traversed by a number of ancient trading routes

GLAISDALE Map ref NZ7705

Visitors will look in vain for the centre of the village, for Glaisdale is a straggling collection of houses clinging to the hillside overlooking the River Esk. Ironstone was worked here; for a time the Angler's Arms was known as the Three Blastfurnaces. However, the Glaisdale mines were never as productive as those of nearby Rosedale.

The valley is very steep-sided here, even with the benefit of hairpin bends motorists have to negotiate the 1-in-3 gradient of Limber Hill on their way up to Egton.

This area is criss-crossed by old tracks – a relic of a time when Glaisdale was a trading centre of some importance. Through East Arncliff Wood (see Walk on page 22) the route is still marked by a line of causeway stones. A number of these paths converge on Beggar's Bridge, a fine packhorse bridge with a romantic story.

It was not easy to cross the Esk at the time when Tom Ferris was courting a local lass who lived on the opposite side of the river. If Tom was not actually a beggar, he was certainly a man of few means. He hoped to win the hand of his beloved by bettering his position, so he enlisted on a ship setting out from Whitby to fight the Spanish Armada, or, as some say, as a privateer or pirate.

When he tried to say farewell to the lady, however, he was thwarted by the River Esk in spate. He sought fame and fortune, and became a successful merchant and Lord Mayor of Hull. Yet he never forgot Glaisdale, and erected the splendid arch of Beggar's Bridge so that no other young lovers should be needlessly parted.

GREAT AYTON   Map ref NZ5610

Great Ayton is bisected by the River Leven, whose clear waters seem almost to deny that the industrial heartland of Middlesbrough is but a short drive away. Behind Great Ayton is the eccentric profile of Roseberry Topping (1,056 feet, 322m), a distinctive landmark for miles around (see page 32).

Great Ayton's two churches lie almost side by side. All Saints' Church is a delightful building dating back to the 12th century, though additions have been made in every succeeding century. The original tower was demolished in 1880. The interior is simple, with walls of rough-hewn stone, and enough original architectural detail to keep lovers of old churches happily engrossed.

The population of Great Ayton grew to the point where the congregation could no longer squeeze into this atmospheric building. Christ Church was consecrated as the new parish church in 1877; fortunately the old church escaped the fate of so many redundant churches, and is now open to the public during the summer months. James Cook's mother and five of his brothers and sisters are buried in churchyard.

Captain James Cook

Fact and fiction are firmly intertwined in a life that has assumed a legendary quality, but we know for certain that James Cook was born in Marton, at that time, 1728, a village, but now a suburb of Middlesbrough. Middlesbrough's Stewart Park now occupies the site of Cook's cottage, and also provides the starting point for the Captain Cook Heritage Trail, which visits places with which he was associated: Marton, Great Ayton, Marske, Staithes and Whitby. The next place, for Cook himself, was Great Ayton where he went to school.

RIVER CROSSINGS
We can only imagine the importance of old river crossings in days gone by. Beggar's Bridge, built in 1619, is now used by walkers; cars cross by a utilitarian metal bridge, while trains on the scenic Esk Valley line pass almost overhead on a viaduct. Here, within the space of a few yards, much of the transport history of the last few centuries is represented.

Roseberry Topping's distinctive conical peak rises beyond Great Ayton

Members of Captain Cook's immediate family are buried in the grounds of the old Church of All Saints

At the age of 16 Cook was apprenticed to a draper in the fishing village of Staithes. He lived and worked on the seafront, near the Cod and Lobster Inn, and would see the ships and fishing cobles coming and going; some landed fish, others came from more distant parts. He was spellbound by the mariners' tales; they held a fascination for the young James Cook that the drapery business failed to match.

The call of the sea proved irresistible. In 1746 Cook went down the coast to Whitby, where he served his maritime apprenticeship under John Walker, a local ship owner and avowed Quaker. Whitby was then the centre of a considerable shipping trade, at its height it was the sixth largest port in the country and a major centre of shipbuilding. Cook lodged with Walker in Grape Lane; many years later this house formed the basis of the Captain Cook Museum.

CAPTAIN COOK'S BIRTHPLACE

Visitors wanting to see the cottage where Captain Cook was born will have a long way to travel. In 1973 a house purporting to be his birthplace was shipped out to Australia, stone by stone, and then reassembled in Melbourne. Marton, in return, received a rock from Point Hicks Hill in Victoria, which was the first landmark to be seen by Captain Cook once his lookout had uttered those immortal words: 'Land ahoy'.

Cook's first experience of seagoing was the distinctly unromantic job of carrying coal to London from Tyneside. He learned his trade in flat-bottomed, wooden sailing ships, known as 'cats'. These ships were well suited to long voyages, and Cook would have seen them setting sail for distant colonies and campaigns.

Cook displayed a particular aptitude for navigation, which he studied in his spare time. In 1755 John Walker offered him the command of his own collier, but Cook decided, instead, to join the Royal Navy. His navigational skills were quickly recognised, and he joined a number of expeditions surveying routes to the newly discovered lands across the Atlantic. It was Cook's investigations of the St Lawrence River that allowed General Wolfe to take Quebec, and ultimately to claim Canada as a British colony.

These successful ventures brought Cook the command of his own ship, and expeditions to Australia, New Zealand and the Pacific. The ships he commanded – the *Endeavour, Resolution* and *Discovery* – were all Whitby-built 'cats'. Some considered them slow and cumbersome, but Cook found them ideal vessels for surveying the unmapped areas of the southern oceans.

The purpose of his first two voyages was to search for

imagined continents in the southern oceans. He succeeded in charting the coastlines of Australia and New Zealand, and even found a cure for scurvy, that scourge of seamen. The third voyage, begun in 1776, was to find a north-west passage from the Atlantic to the Pacific. Though this objective remained unrealised, Cook did succeed in mapping previously uncharted areas of the Pacific.

This epic voyage proved to be his last. In 1779 he anchored off the Sandwich Islands (now known as Hawaii) to pick up essential supplies. Some members of his crew who went ashore were taken by local natives. It was during attempts to rescue his men that Cook met his end – by being bludgeoned to death.

Great Ayton's claim to fame is that James Cook received his early education (between 1736 and 1741) at the village's Postgate School, reached by walking along the River Leven towards High Green. The school is now a museum dedicated to his illustrious life and travels. The upstairs rooms chart – literally – his three great voyages around the southern oceans. His task was to search for trading routes, and for continents whose very existence was merely conjecture.

In those days, before photography, an on board artist was commissioned to produce pictures of the people and places they visited. One picture on display shows a sandy bay fringed with palm trees. Cook's ship is at anchor, dwarfing a flotilla of tiny craft filled with islanders. Such pictures were widely distributed as prints; the exotic subjects proved irresistible.

A monument to Captain Cook, 50 feet (15.25m) high, set up in 1827 on nearby Easby Moor, can be seen for miles around.

POSTGATE SCHOOL
Founded in 1704, the school was designed to take eight poor boys of the town, but was soon accommodating up to 30 boys and girls. The school fees for the young James Cook were paid for by the lord of the manor, Thomas Skottowe, by whom Cook's father was employed. The school is now home to the Captain Cook Museum.

Grand façades decorate the cottages on High Green, one of two greens in the village

Old Trackways through Glaisdale

A beautiful old bridge leads on to a paved causeway, once used by trains of packhorse ponies transporting goods from town to town. An exploration of the wooded Esk Valley is followed by a walk over breezy moorland.

Time: 3 hours. Distance: 4½ miles (7.2km).
Location: 8 miles (12.9km) southwest of Whitby.
Start: Park at Beggar's Bridge, at the bottom of the hill between Glaisdale and Egton Bridge, or at Glaisdale railway station.
(OS grid ref: NZ784055.)
OS Map: Outdoor Leisure 27 (North York Moors – Eastern area) 1:25,000.
See Key to Walks on page 123.

ROUTE DIRECTIONS

From **Beggar's Bridge** walk beneath the railway line, over a little footbridge next to a ford and climb steep steps up into East Arncliff Wood. The path quickly levels out, offering delightful views down to the River Esk. The path descends to river level,

and the walk continues on a splendid **causeway**.

The path goes through coppiced woodland before reaching a road, where you bear right, uphill. Pass a house called The Delves and continue up and around a hairpin bend. At the top of the hill take a footpath to the left. There are two gates here, take the one on the right. Continue on the path downhill between hedgerows into a clearing. Bear left and follow the yellow arrows to a stile. Cross the farm track behind The Delves farm and continue in the same direction, through a gate waymarked 'Hall Grange'.

Go over a wall-stile and continue downhill, following a tall hedge, to cross the footbridge over Butter Beck. Climb uphill, through a gate, following the sign with a yellow arrow, and turn left along the field edge. The path crosses a beck, then climbs up to a stile at the top of a field where it joins a bridleway, which you follow to the right. Soon pass Hall Grange Farm and its many outbuildings. As the track rises there are open fields to the left and woodland to the right. Shortly the view is of moorland, with extensive views down into Butter Beck Valley.

The track continues almost to the door of Grange Head Farm, but then skirts the farm buildings. Bear right, through a gate, and follow an indistinct field path towards another farm on the hillside ahead. Negotiate a gate, a farm track bridge, another gate and the edge of a wood to reach a footbridge and then it is a steep climb up to

The well-worn stones of the old causeway will keep your feet dry through East Arncliff Wood

Lodge Hill Farm. Go through a gate and walk straight through the farmyard and bear left on to a good track.

The track goes through another farmyard. When the track forks take the left fork through a gate. On reaching a road, look for a footpath sign across the road, slightly to the right: go through a gate and along a track. Soon the village of Glaisdale can be seen on the horizon. Walk through scrubland of old iron workings until you reach a more substantial track between walls. Walk right, downhill, along the track into woodland and return to the River Esk, its trio of bridges, and your starting point.

tracks around Glaisdale confirms the village's importance as a trading centre in days gone by.

The pleasing arch of Beggar's Bridge was built by Tom Ferris, a successful son of Glaisdale

POINTS OF INTEREST

Beggar's Bridge

These days we take river crossings for granted, but the elegant arch of Beggar's Bridge is a potent reminder of earlier times. Built by Tom Ferris, a Glaisdale man (see page 18), the bridge still bears his initials and the date: 1619.

Causeway

Part of our walk through East Arnecliff Wood follows causeway lines of well-fitting stones. Some of these causeways were constructed to provide access between monastic communities and outlying lands and granges. Others, usually keeping to the higher ground, were for the lines of packhorse ponies carrying all manner of goods in pannier bags, including fish from the sea, and salt to the ports to preserve fish. These causeways, principally of the 17th and 18th centuries, offered routes through what was often an inhospitable moorland landscape. The proliferation of these paved

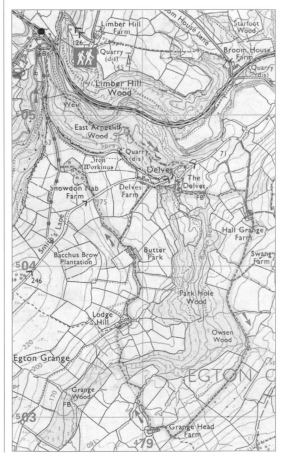

THE RAIL TRAIL
The Rail Trail extends from Grosmont to Goathland, so it can easily be combined with a trip along this most scenic of railway lines (the Rail Trail booklet suggests the train journey to Goathland followed by a walk back to Grosmont). The 3-mile (4.8km) footpath follows the route of the original section of line between the two villages, via Beck Hole, as laid in 1836.

GROSMONT Map ref NZ8305

Built largely to house those who worked on the Pickering–Whitby railway line that splits the village in two, Grosmont was originally, and unimaginatively, called 'Tunnel'. With its terraced houses and mining spoil, Grosmont presents a more industrial face to the world than the other villages of the Esk Valley. Indeed, it was while excavating the Pickering–Whitby line, in 1835, that the richest ironstone deposits were first discovered. Once completed, the railway was convenient for the delivery of ironstone to ships in Whitby harbour. By the middle of the 19th century, Grosmont was a major supplier of ironstone to the ironmasters' furnaces on the Rivers Tyne and Tees.

The name 'Grosmont' recalls the 13th-century Grandmontine Priory, founded here by French monks. The priory is long gone, its place taken by Priory Farm and its stonework salvaged for secular buildings.

The Pickering–Whitby line was built in 1836 after consulting George Stephenson, who came to the project straight from the triumphant success of his Stockton–Darlington railway. The line was closed, controversially, in 1965 by Beeching's infamous axe. It was reborn 8 years later, thanks to massive support by railway enthusiasts, as the North Yorkshire Moors Railway, a recreational line manned by volunteers. There is nothing amateurish about the enterprise, though, for they maintain a regular timetable, come rain, come shine, and even leaves on the line.

Railway buffs can admire the gleaming old locomotives getting up steam at Grosmont station, which has been convincingly restored to how it may have looked a century ago; there is also public access to the engine sheds. The full story of the line can be found on page 106.

Grosmont is the northern terminus of the railway, offering connections with Northern Spirit services on the Esk Valley line between Middlesbrough and Whitby. It is a junction of roads and rivers, too, with the Murk Esk draining into the River Esk.

GUISBOROUGH Map ref NZ6015

Guisborough's broad main street and cobbled verges indicate that markets have been held here for centuries. The old market cross is topped by a sundial. Today the market traders put up their stalls on Thursdays and Saturdays, drawing their customers from many of the villages on the edge of the moors.

Like its close neighbour, Stokesley, the town's status has changed in recent years. Until the boundary changes of 1974, Guisborough was the capital town of the Cleveland district, which formed part of the North Riding of Yorkshire. Those reorganisations shifted the town into the county of Cleveland, but it has now been brought back into North Yorkshire.

Beyond the main street and the market cross is the largely 15th-century Church of St Nicholas, where a cenotaph reinforces the links between the local de Bruce family and the Bruces of Scotland. Robert the Bruce's grandfather is buried near by at Gisborough Priory.

The huge east window of the ruined Augustinian priory still stands to its full height of nearly 71 feet (20m), gazing out across farmland. To wander around the evocative ruins is to escape immediately from the bustle of Guisborough's busy streets. The priory was built in the early 14th century by Robert de Brus, who was related to the Scottish king, Robert the Bruce. In their contemplation of the life to come, the monks did not neglect to lay up their treasures on earth, and by the time of the Dissolution they had become one of the richest communities in the north.

Nearby Gisborough Hall sits in beautiful wooded surroundings. The hall was built by Sir Thomas Challoner, whose son began the mining of alum on the moors in about 1600. The industry proved vital to the moorland economy for the following three centuries. He stole the secrets of alum mining and processing from the Pope, no less, who had enjoyed a near-monopoly in the alum industry. He even persuaded some of the Pope's miners to accompany him back to England to begin alum mining on the moors. For this impertinence the Challoner family was excommunicated from the Catholic Church.

Just a mile (1.6km) out of town, on the A173 in the direction of Skelton, is Tocketts Mill. The water of Tocketts Beck still turns the waterwheel of this fine old flour mill, and on certain milling days the restored building is open to the public.

A HAUNTED PRIORY
Gisborough Priory is thought to be haunted by the ghost of a black-cowled monk. It is said that he revisits his old home every year, letting down a drawbridge over a moat – both of which have long since disappeared.

The dramatic priory ruins stand in the grounds of Gisborough Hall

ALUM MINING

Alum was valued for its ability to fix dyes in the textile industries; other uses included applications in leather tanning, and the manufacture of candles and parchment. The availability of locally mined alum meant that the tanning and dyeing industries had a reliable supply, at just a fifth of the price per ton they paid for imported alum. Alum was mined on the moors, and at Kettleness the shales were shovelled out of the cliffs, piled into huge mounds on top of brushwood, which was then set alight. Urine, brought in as ballast in barrels from the public houses of London, was added to the burnt shale, and this solution, first boiled, then cooled, produced crystals of alum.

THE KETTLENESS BOGGLES

It's hardly surprising that Kettleness had its boggles; these unruly little goblins turn up repeatedly in folk tales from the moors. No records exist of what the Kettleness boggles looked like, for they lived in caves by the sea, way down below the village, and no-one was so foolhardy as to venture there. But once a week the boggles could be heard washing their clothes in a tub, and beating them with paddles.

Kettleness points a precarious finger of exposed rock into the North Sea, opposite

KETTLENESS AND GOLDSBOROUGH

Map ref NZ8414

Travellers on the A174 between Staithes and Whitby are seldom tempted to take one of the roads to the left, before arriving in the roadside village of Lythe. The signpost indicates Goldsborough and Kettleness, a pair of hamlets whose history is by no means as tranquil as they appear today.

The handful of houses clustered together in Kettleness look as if they could fall off the cliff top at any minute. That's precisely what happened in 1829, when a landslip devastated the entire community. Fortunately, the villagers had enough warning of the impending disaster to vacate their properties and to be rescued by a ship waiting for them offshore. But why bother to rebuild the village on such an exposed site? The answer can be found by taking a path down on to Kettleness Point, a rocky promontory that supports barely a blade of grass. Here are the remains of productive alum mines.

How precarious a living alum mining provided can be appreciated by the fact that the foundations of many of the mining buildings end suddenly at the cliff edge. The folk of Kettleness lost their livelihood, and their village, in the landslip of 1829; the mining and processing of alum was back in full swing within five years.

Today, Kettleness Point is a dramatic moonscape, offering nesting sites for thousands of seabirds and, to the north, a view of Runswick Bay. The promontory forms part of the Heritage Coast: a sort of linear national park which aims to preserve the undeveloped coastlines with some of the most spectacular scenery along the east coast. Special protection is now given to the 36-mile (57.6km) stretch of coastline between Saltburn and Scalby Ness, on the outskirts of Scarborough.

Goldsborough, just over half a mile (800m) inland, was the site of a 4th-century Roman signal station. The Roman road commonly known as Wade's Causeway (see page 92) was probably built to link the Roman settlement at Malton with the signal stations dotted at regular intervals along the coast. However, all that remains to be seen here are some grassy earthworks sited some 219 yards (200m) from the road between Goldsborough and Kettleness. Excavations early in the 20th century produced a number of interesting Roman finds, which suggested that the signal station might have ended its days by being suddenly ransacked. Near by is a modern coastguard station.

The giant Wade, whose moorland exploits were legion, is, according to legend, buried at Goldsborough. A pair of standing stones – one by Goldsborough Lane, the other adjacent to the A174 at East Barnby – are known as Wade's Stones and are said to mark the position of his head and feet. The stones are, however, more than half a mile (800m) apart, which would have made him stand out even at a giants' convention.

🚗

Around the Cleveland Hills and Esk Dale

This 60-mile (96.5-km) route skirts the Cleveland Hills, passes high cliffs and fishing villages, before exploring the more intimate landscape of the delightful Esk Valley. Staithes, Whitby and the villages along the Esk Valley are well worth exploring, and Lealholm makes an ideal picnic spot. The drive starts and ends at Great Ayton, a handsome town where Captain James Cook spent much of his boyhood. Houses overlook the River Leven, and rearing up behind them is Great Ayton's 'miniature Matterhorn', Roseberry Topping.

ROUTE DIRECTIONS

See Key to Car Tours on page 122.

Leave Great Ayton along the A173, signposted 'Whitby'. Roseberry Topping is the hill, with a 'bite' taken out of its summit due to ironstone mining. Turn right at a roundabout towards Whitby on the A171. Keep straight on at the next roundabout, on the outskirts of Guisborough, but bear left at the next roundabout, on to the A173, signposted 'Redcar & Saltburn'. Cross another roundabout almost immediately, and pass restored Tocketts Mill. Bear left at traffic lights in Skelton (signposted 'Whitby'), soon to go right at a roundabut on the A174, signed 'Brotton & Whitby'. Cross over four roundabouts, bear right at the fifth, signposted 'Whitby', and go through Carlin How, to get your first sight of the sea.

Follow Whitby signs (A174), down hairpin bends near Skinningrove, where the Tom Leonard Mining Museum can be found. Go through Loftus.

Sea views open out as the fishing village of Staithes appears on the horizon. Pass the unsightly bulk of Boulby Potash Mine, and then Staithes. The view from the road does not prepare you for the delights of the old part of the village. Leave your car at the top of the village, and explore the village and harbour on foot.

The A174 continues through rolling farmland past Lythe and its prominent church. **Whitby Abbey** can be seen on the horizon as you drop steeply down into Sandsend. Take great care on Lythe Bank, there have been many runaways here. After Whitby golf club you approach the town itself. Turn right following signs for the A171 signposted 'Scarborough and Pickering' then right again at a garage. Take the left-hand fork soon after and turn left at a roundabout to arrive at some lights. Turn left still following signs for the A171 'Scarborough and Robin Hood's Bay'.

Cross the River Esk on an elevated bridge, with views over Whitby's harbour and Marina. Immediately over the bridge there is a road to your left, your route if you want to see the church and abbey at close quarters. Otherwise your road is to the right, directly opposite, and signposted, rather unpromisingly, 'Larpool Industrial Estate'. This unclassified road takes you to the village of Ruswarp, and the River Esk. From here you will keep in close proximity to the river for most of the way back to Great Ayton.

Turn right to cross Ruswarp's river bridge and adjacent railway line, then turn immediately left on the B1410 to Sleights. Follow the River Esk; go left at a T-junction on to the A169, signposted 'Pickering'. When you are almost through the village of Sleights, look out for a road on the right, signed 'Grosmont' and 'Egton'.

There are delightful views into Esk Dale before dropping down into Grosmont, where

the **North Yorkshire Moors Railway** connects with the Middlesbrough–Whitby branch line services. Carry on to Egton where you take the left fork, downhill towards Egton Bridge. Turn right after the church, signposted Glaisdale. Climb steeply to a T-junction; turn left here and negotiate the precipitous 1-in-3 (33%) Limber Hill down to the ancient stone arch of Beggar's Bridge that once carried trains of packhorse ponies over the River Esk.

Climb up through the straggle of houses in Glaisdale; signs are now for Lealholm. Turn right at a T-junction to descend into Lealholm. With its arched bridge, stepping stones and grassy river banks, this is one of the prettiest villages along the Esk Valley.

Cross the bridge over the River Esk, and take a turn immediately to the left, signposted 'Danby'. Pass graceful Duck Bridge and the National Park's **Moors**

Centre, bearing left to Danby village. Keep straight ahead at the crossroads, signed 'Castleton'. In Castleton village, turn right halfway up the hill, signposted 'Guisborough'. Cross the River Esk once again, to climb up on to open moorland. At the first junction by the White Cross base go left on a road signposted 'Commondale'

This drive takes in some of the most attractive scenery around Esk Dale

and 'Stokesley'.

Pass through Commondale, as fine moorland views open up. Continue through Kildale, take two right turns following the signposts 'Great Ayton' and the start of the tour.

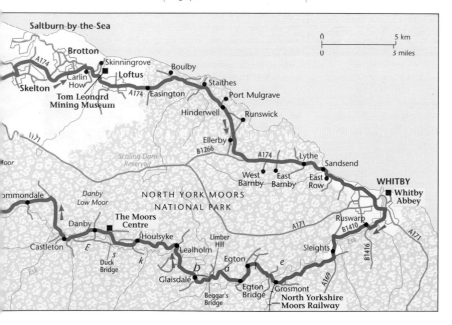

Kildale lies to the southeast of Great Ayton, on the edge of the Cleveland Hills

KILDALE Map ref NZ6009

This little moorland village has a station on the Esk Valley line between Middlesbrough and Whitby. Completed in 1865, the Esk Valley line had to make a total of 17 river crossings between the stations at Kildale and Grosmont. It was fortunate to escape Beeching's axe, and is still a valued amenity for locals and visitors alike.

St Cuthbert's Church is reached via a footbridge over the railway. A hoard of Viking relics, including swords and battleaxes, was found here in 1868 when the church was renovated. These finds show that Kildale is an ancient settlement, a notion reinforced by earthworks and other finds. A mound, cut into by the railway line, is now the only clue that Kildale once had a motte and bailey castle. This was one of the many strongholds owned by the Percy family, whose name is kept alive by names such as Percy Cross and Percy Rigg, high on the moors. There have been many attempts to find an origin for the name 'Kildale', which applies to both the village and the valley through which the River Leven flows. 'Kil' is probably a corruption of 'Ketil', a personal name.

The Cleveland Way drops down briefly from the moors, to pass through Kildale. If you walk the route going north you will arrive on the breezy heights of Easby Moor where a monument, put up in 1827, commemorates the life and exploits of Captain James Cook. From here you can enjoy panoramic views down over Great Ayton, where the young James Cook spent his formative years.

Kildale's rights of way were taken from an old map

QUOITS

The game of quoits is played in many villages along the Esk Valley. It is neither as simple, nor as easy, as might be supposed. The target, about ten yards away, is a metal pin set into a square yard of clay. The projectile is a heavy iron ring – with contoured edges like a saucer with a hole cut out of the middle. The object, of course, is to throw the heavy quoit over the peg, but there's much more to it than that, as you'll discover if you watch seasoned players.

that marked only three, so there are few of the field paths that typify nearby villages. The road between Kildale and Westerdale offers splendid moorland scenery, and the watersplash over Baysdale Beck is a popular spot for a picnic.

LEALHOLM   Map ref NZ7607

The River Esk runs through the narrow, wooded confines of Crunkly Gill, one of the many gorges carved by Ice-Age meltwaters, before flowing through Lealholm's grassy banks. This attractive little village, astride a bend in the river, acts as a magnet for visitors. Lealholm was a favourite place, too, for Canon Atkinson, vicar of nearby Danby (see page 13), who wrote lyrically about the village in his book *Forty Years in a Moorland Parish*, 'Elsewhere you must go in search of beautiful views; here they offer themselves to be looked at'.

The river is spanned by a well-proportioned bridge of peach-coloured stone; a few yards away is a line of stepping stones, they seem to have an irresistible attraction for small children. Beyond the bridge is the Board Inn, offering refreshment and another vantage point from which to gaze down over the Esk.

Lealholm boasts no buildings of great note; visitors come here largely because the green is common land where they can roam at will and spread a picnic rug. On a sunny summer's day the river bank is a relaxing spot; greedy mallard ducks will eagerly dispose of any leftover sandwiches. Tearooms and craft shops complete the picture. The National Park Authority has bowed to visitor pressure by providing a car park.

Lealholm can be grouped with other beauty spots, such as Goathland, Hutton-le-Hole and Thornton-le-Dale, as places best avoided on sunny Bank Holidays, unless you really love crowds. Apart from that caveat, it's a delightful place.

A SCENIC ROUTE

If you drive south from Lealholm, you have a choice of minor roads – left to Glaisdale, straight on for a moorland drive 'over the tops' and on into Rosedale, or you may be intrigued by a sign on the right, to Fryup Dale. You have a further choice, Great Fryup Dale or Little Fryup Dale. The mellifluous names have a more mundane origin, 'Friga' is an Old English personal name, while 'up' simply means a valley. A drive around either of Friga's valleys makes a pleasant detour from the main Esk Valley. Great Fryup Dale is a broad green valley, dotted with farms and divided up by field walls that climb straight up to the moor-top. The road makes a circuit of the valley, taking you back into Lealholm.

The sport of quoit-throwing is taken very seriously in Lealholm

ROSEBERRY'S PROFILE
The distinctive profile of
Roseberry Topping has been
likened to a Roman nose and
a shark's fin. It is certainly a
reminder of how the hand of
man can have a dramatic
effect upon the landscape.

ROSEBERRY TOPPING   Map ref NZ5813

Roseberry Topping, just north of Great Ayton, is
Cleveland's own 'Matterhorn'. Its height, just 1,056 feet
(322m), hardly qualifies it as a major peak, yet it is a
prominent landmark for miles around, standing aloof
from the surrounding Cleveland Hills.

To see Roseberry Topping as nature intended, as an
almost symmetrical cone, you will have to look at old
prints. As soon as its mineral wealth was realised, it was
exploited for its alum, iron-ore, jet and roadstone. So
heavily was it mined and quarried that a great chunk of
the hill came away in a landslip, making the residents of
the nearby village of Newton under Roseberry fear for
their lives.

This landslip created the distinctive profile we see
today. Climb to the top and to the northwest is the
industrial heartland of Middlesbrough, its urban sprawl
creeping inexorably outwards; to the south are
panoramic views across the moors.

Roseberry Topping's prominence has made it an
important landmark for millennia. There is some
evidence that it was even an object of veneration.
'Roseberry' is a corruption of the old Viking name,
'Othenesberg', (that is, Odin's Hill), indicating it was
probably sacred to the Danish god of creation. 'Topping',
also of Scandinavian origin, means a peak. Seventeenth-
century references have it as 'Osbury Toppyne', at a time
when it was one of the many beacon hills on which fires
were built – to be set alight if the Spanish Armada were
sighted at sea.

*Roseberry Topping's curious
peak is a landmark for miles
around*

RUNSWICK BAY Map ref NZ8016

A long arc of sandy beach extends south from the houses of Runswick, to form one of the loveliest bays on the Yorkshire coast. There is shelter here from blustery winds and high seas; over the centuries many a ship's captain has been relieved to find safe harbour here.

The cliffs that protect the bay take a battering each winter, whole chunks can disappear in a storm. This coast has always been eroded; sea defences have only a limited effect and are expensive to maintain. Since medieval times the coastline has changed dramatically, with inland villages creeping ever closer to the shore, and many coastal villages sliding into the sea. You only have to look at old maps to realise that the 'lost' villages of Yorkshire's coast can be counted in scores.

Runswick fell into the sea in the year 1682. Fortunately no lives were lost; the villagers knew their fate and were evacuated. The Runswick of today comprises a pleasing collection of red-roofed cottages, clinging limpet-like to the cliff, connected by steps and alleyways. The sheltering bay, good soil and south-facing aspect make Runswick a suntrap; in spring and summer the little terraced gardens make a colourful picture. The whitewashed house prominently sited on the headland was the coastguard's cottage.

A few fishing cobles are still lined up above the high watermark, though today your neighbour is more likely to be a holiday-maker than a fisherman. The lifeboat is always at the ready, however; ships can still be caught out by sudden changes in the weather. In 1901 a storm blew up while most of the fishing boats were at sea. The women of the village launched the lifeboat and thereby saved many lives.

Lobster boats are stored high and dry above the shore at pretty Runswick Bay

HOB HOLES

The caves at the far end of Runswick Bay are the result of jet mining and natural erosion by the sea. They were called the Hob Holes, and were supposed to be the home of hobs, Yorkshire's own 'little people'. Traditionally good-tempered, unless wronged by thoughtless humans, the hobs had a particular skill – being able to cure the whooping cough. Mothers would bring their children in the hope that the hobs would oblige. As in many of these old stories, there may be more than a grain of truth, as the fumes produced when jet was burned were thought to have had beneficial effects on bronchial conditions.

Staithes and Port Mulgrave

An undemanding exploration of a fascinating stretch of coastline. Port Mulgrave evokes a long-lost industry, while Staithes remains the epitome of a North Yorkshire fishing village.

Time: 2½ hours. Distance: 4 miles (6.4km).
Location: 8 miles (12.9km) northwest of Whitby.
Start: Turn off the A174, signposted 'Staithes'; in 200 yards (183m) turn right at a mini-roundabout and follow the signs into the car park (pay-and-display during the summer).
(OS grid ref: NZ782185.)
OS Map: Outdoor Leisure 27 (North York Moors – Eastern area) 1:25,000.
See Key to Walks on page 123.

ROUTE DIRECTIONS

Walk down the steep lane into the old part of **Staithes**, turn right just after the Cod and Lobster, and walk up steep Church Street, passing the mission church of St Peter the Fisherman. When the road ends at the top, take the path which continues uphill. When the path forks, keep left, signposted 'Cleveland Way'. Pass a farm and continue along a path between fences. The path continues to rise to Beacon Hill; from here you walk along the cliff top. Enjoy the sea views, but take care as the cliff edge is unfenced. When the path deviates inland over Beacon Hill, follow it to **Port Mulgrave**.

A path leads down to the harbour – a steep and hard pull back up – otherwise continue to join a road and walk away from the cliff-top path. Pass houses, and turn right at a telephone box into open fields. Opposite a caravan site, turn left at a footpath sign, and cross the middle of a field. At a stile (lovely views from here) continue downhill to a road. Cross the road and turn right into a layby and shortly take a stile and steps to the left. Skirt, then enter woodland and continue on the path downhill to a footbridge. Walk uphill to the right through coppiced woodland to emerge into open scrubland with new conifer plantings.

The path leads downhill, through woods, to a caravan site. Cross a bridge and join a cinder track which soon enters Dalehouse, a cluster of buildings where a number of streams combine to form Staithes Beck. Turn right at the road and continue uphill to the main A174. Cross the road and walk right, to continue on the road into Staithes village and the car park.

POINTS OF INTEREST

Staithes
Staithes (see page 37) still looks substantially the same as it did in 1745 when the young James Cook was apprenticed to a draper in

The Cleveland Way crosses the hills above Port Mulgrave

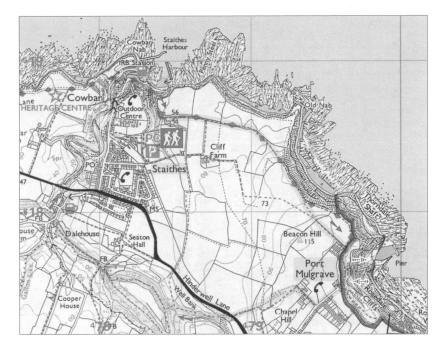

the village. The draper's shop was lost to the ravages of the North Sea, a fate shared by many other houses in the village.

The village is a delight to explore; its position, wedged between cliffs, led to imaginative house building. The harbour and the mouth of Cowbar Beck are still filled with fishing cobles. These days they go to sea mainly for crabs and lobsters which can be bought in the village shops.

Port Mulgrave

While Staithes is the archetypal fishing village, and achingly photogenic to boot, penny-plain Port Mulgrave owed its existence to the mining of iron ore, an industry that was to become vital to the shipbuilders on Tyneside. There were productive mines in many places near the coast, such as Skinningrove, Boulby and Grinkle; the main problem was the transport of iron to the Rivers Tees and Tyne. When tides and weather allowed, flat-bottomed ships could be pulled up on to the beaches, but the search for a more reliable method of transport led to the building, in 1855, of a little harbour at Port Mulgrave.

The iron ore was brought from the mines to the harbour via a mile-long (1.6km) tunnel and loaded into waiting ships by means of a complex system of tramways and gantries. All are now gone, as mining ceased 60 years ago, and the tunnel blocked up, leaving just a harbour wall as a reminder of a bygone industry.

Cobbles line a winding old street near the harbour at Staithes

LEWIS CARROLL
It was while strolling along the beach at Sandsend that Lewis Carroll first had the idea for his surreal poem about the Walrus and the Carpenter. You can follow in his footsteps, at low tide it is a splendid walk of about 2½ miles (4km) along the beach to Whitby.

SANDSEND   Map ref NZ6812

The approach to Sandsend along the A174 is steeply downhill from Lythe, views open up of a long sandy beach and, in the distance, Whitby Abbey dominates the horizon. Here is a placename that, for once, needs no interpretation. Sandsend marks the northern end of a sandy beach, one of the best on Yorkshire's coast, stretching down as far as Whitby harbour.

The village has been a hive of industry for centuries; the Romans had a cement works here. More recently the bare outcrop of Sandsend Ness was mined for alum; it is still bare today, due to the heaps of mining waste. Remarkably, these mines were worked continuously for two and a half centuries. When Yorkshire's coast had its railway, Sandsend was overlooked by a long viaduct, raised up above the red-tiled rooftops on tall pillars. Both the line and the viaduct disappeared in the 1960s: more's the pity, many may think.

The Sandsend of today is a much more tranquil spot, with Sandsend Ness sheltering the village from the battering of the north wind and heavy seas. Mickleby Beck and East Row Beck reach the sea at Sandsend a mere 97 feet (30m) apart; instead of staring out to sea most of the cottages in the village are clustered either side of their banks. Paths accompany both of these valleys into lovely Mulgrave Woods, a traditional broadleaved woodland.

On the narrow ridge between these valleys is Mulgrave Castle, a fine Georgian pile. Guests at the castle included William Wordsworth and Charles Dickens; both wrote glowingly about the fine views to be had from here. In the grounds are the evocative, ivy-clad ruins of a much earlier castle, dating from the 13th century.

Looking along the glorious bay at Sandsend, with the stark ruins of Whitby Abbey on the horizon

STAITHES Map ref NZ7818

It is easy to miss the Staithes turning off the main A174 coast road. Nor is the first sight of the village very promising. You have to drive half a mile (800m), park in the pay-and-display car park and proceed on foot if you want to see why Staithes is so special.

This most perfectly preserved of Yorkshire fishing villages is divided into two by Cowbar Beck and the steep-sided gorge through which it runs. For centuries the people of Staithes have had to cope with the twin problems of an inhospitable site and the ravages of the North Sea. They have made their living from the sea, while always respecting its awesome power.

The Staithes we see today is a village that would be immediately familiar to the young James Cook, who spent an impatient 18 months working at the counter of a draper's shop in the village before realising his ambition to go to sea. The whitewashed houses, red-pantiled roofs, fishing cobles and lobster pots would make him feel at home.

It may seem that time has stood still, but the battering from the sea has been relentless. Despite the shelter of its steep cliffs, Staithes has lost many buildings to stormy seas. The little draper's shop was washed away; a house near the Cod and Lobster pub bears a commemorative plaque but has been rebuilt since James Cook lived and worked here. The pub itself backs uncompromisingly on to the harbour wall and has suffered more than its fair share of storm damage, having been rebuilt three times – the last occasion being as recently as 1953.

On a sunny summer's day it is hard to imagine such

Old cottages perch precipitously on the slopes down into Staithes

VIEWPOINTS ABOVE STAITHES

A walk of less than an hour from the village of Staithes will offer a variety of viewpoints, looking down on the random patchwork of red-tiled roofs from the cliff tops – known as Cowbar Nab and Old Nab – on either side of the gorge, connected by the arch of a footbridge.

A veritable web of mooring lines secure the little cobles in Staithes harbour

A MAJOR FISHING PORT

Sleepy Staithes has known busier days. During the first half of the 19th century as many as 300 men went to sea in the distinctive fishing cobles, to net mostly cod, haddock and mackerel. These small craft, with a crew of three, were often accompanied by larger yawls. Fish could be transferred from the cobles into the larger vessels for easier transport back to harbour.

Fish was dispatched from Staithes all over the country; teams of packhorses were maintained to do nothing more than carry some of each day's catch to York market. The death-knell of Staithes as a major fishing port came with the introduction of the steam trawler.

destruction. You would have to make your visit in winter, when a strong northeasterly gale is blowing, and the waves are hammering relentlessly against the harbour wall, to understand why the people of Staithes have earned a reputation for self-reliance. To have maintained a viable community here, despite the obvious drawbacks, is remarkable in itself.

Fishing has long provided a living, albeit a precarious one, for the men of Staithes. The little harbour, and the mouth of Cowbar Beck, are still full of the traditional fishing cobles – whose slightly upturned prows betray their Nordic origins. But today they go to sea mainly for crabs and lobsters; you can buy them freshly caught at shops in the village.

Painters and photographers are attracted in droves to the village. There are echoes of some of the more picturesque fishing villages of Cornwall, but few communities in the country can boast a more extraordinary setting than Staithes. The village used to have a railway station; both station and line are gone, leaving just the trackbed and the stanchions of the old viaduct over the gorge as reminders of the scenic line from Saltburn to Scarborough. Parts of the trackbed are used in our Walks on pages 90 and 110.

To the north of Staithes are Boulby Cliffs. At more than 650 feet (200m) they are the highest, if not the most dramatic, on the east coast and offer excellent views. Close by is Boulby Potash Mine. The extent of the mining operation here can be gauged by the fact that tunnels extend almost 3 miles (4.8km) out under the sea.

UGTHORPE   Map ref NZ7911

Never a contender for the title of prettiest name, the moorland village of Ugthorpe is nevertheless an interesting spot. The name may derive from Ligulph, a Saxon landowner.

Nicholas Postgate, the 'Martyr of the Moors', was born in 1597 in the Esk Dale village of Egton Bridge (see page 14). At this time Roman Catholicism was banned in England, so when Postgate decided to become a Catholic priest he knew he had chosen a hazardous profession. He trained for the ministry in France, and then returned to his native Yorkshire. For many years he served as chaplain for well-heeled Catholic families, before returning to the moors at the age of 60.

A thatched cottage in Ugthorpe was where Father Postgate found a haven. He travelled the moorland tracks, often disguised as a beggar or gardener, risking his life to take the comfort of the Mass to isolated farmsteads. Remarkably, with persecution rife, he even managed to make new converts to the faith.

While the authorities turned a blind eye to some of these activities, they reacted savagely to the so-called Popish Plot: an attempt, in 1678, to usurp the throne of Charles II. Catholic sympathisers were rounded up and rewards were offered to informers. The £20 bounty on Father Postgate's head proved an irresistible temptation to a local man, John Reeves. The priest was arrested while baptising a baby at Ugglebarnby, and taken to York to stand trial.

Despite his venerable years, he was an old man in his 80s, Father Postgate was sentenced to death by being hanged, drawn and quartered. He met his end with great dignity, forgiving those who had testified against him. Soon afterwards, the body of John Reeves was found in the river; he seems, like Judas, to have taken his own life. Ugthorpe's Catholic church dates from 1850, when such anti-Catholic witch-hunts were but a distant memory.

'SAFE HOUSES'
A number of wealthy landowners on the moors professed the Catholic faith, and offered 'safe houses' where Father Postgate could hold his services in secret. Priest holes can also be found in other buildings around Ugthorpe.

Tiny windows on a delightful cottage in Ugthorpe reveal the building's age

FRANK MEADOW SUTCLIFFE
Photographer Frank Meadow
Sutcliffe's bread-and-butter
work was portraiture. But his
passion was Whitby itself. He
used a huge and cumbersome
view camera, which precluded
any notion of candid
photography, to photograph
the town. He stage-managed
his compositions (even paying
some of his subjects to ensure
co-operation) to produce
lustrous images of gnarled
fishermen, street traders and
grubby urchins – with the tall-
masted sailing ships and
Whitby harbour as
picturesque backdrops.
(Continued on next page)

*An early morning in Whitby
harbour*

WHITBY Map ref NZ8910

Those who take a leisurely stroll along the harbour front
may be mistaken for thinking of Whitby as just another
resort devoted to the arcane delights of bingo,
amusement arcades, candyfloss and 'Kiss Me Quick' hats.
But Whitby has a great deal more to offer, enough to
keep the most demanding visitor interested for some
time. For Whitby has a long, illustrious and genuine
history as one of the country's most important seaports,
and the town can claim associations with a remarkable
variety of historical figures.

The setting itself is dramatic, Whitby's houses clinging
to the steep slopes either side of the River Esk. A good
overview of the town can be enjoyed from the elevated
bridge that now carries through traffic on the A171 at a
convenient distance from the town's narrow streets.
From this vantage point you can see the Esk broaden
into a large marina full of yachts. Beyond the swing
bridge is the harbour, overlooked spectacularly on the
southern flank by St Mary's Church and the ruined
abbey – a landmark for miles around.

The scene is one of bustle and activity. Whitby has
thrived when other fishing towns and villages have
declined, and new building projects emphasise that the
town is looking to the future as well as the past.

Whitby has always gazed out to sea. For centuries the town was isolated from the rest of the county by poor roads and the wild expanse of moorland that surround it on three sides. Yet by the 18th century it had risen to the status of a major port, with shipbuilding, fishing and whaling contributing to a maritime prosperity that lasted until well into the early years of the 20th century. The fine Georgian houses at the west end of the town, built by wealthy shipbuilders and fleet owners, attest to this success.

Elsewhere the more traditional cottages, whitewashed and with red-tiled roofs, housed the fishermen. Space was at a premium, so their houses were built in close proximity, mostly up the steep inclines on the eastern side of the Esk. They are linked by ginnels and steps, which beg to be explored. Be sure to leave your car in one of the long-stay car parks near the marina; Whitby's narrow streets were definitely not built with motor traffic in mind.

The large harbour is still at the heart of the town, though today there are more pleasure craft passing the breakwaters than fishing cobles. Whitby traditionally offered the only safe harbour between the Rivers Tyne and Humber. The North Yorkshire coast is notoriously prone to storms, and many ships have been wrecked, unable to find sanctuary in time.

Whitby prospered during the 17th and 18th centuries with the mining and refining of alum – a vital ingredient in the dyeing of wool. Coal was brought here to fire the cauldrons that separated alum from rock, and stone was needed for building; this increase in trade required the building of a better harbour.

In 1753 a company was set up in the town to

A splendid line of Georgian terraces takes full advantage of both morning sunshine and the harbour view

(Continued from previous page)
It isn't merely the patina of age that makes Sutcliffe's pictures so beguiling. Everyone he photographed may be long gone, but the locations can still be seen today. Despite the cars, the cafés and the candyfloss, there is a continuing thread that links the Whitby of today to the Whitby that Sutcliffe knew so well. At the Sutcliffe Gallery you can find framed prints of his evocative photographs, all taken from the original negatives.

The famous Whitby jet can be found on sale in the shops along the steep, winding streets of the town

WHITBY JET

Whitby jet has been used to make jewellery since the Bronze Age, but it was popularised by Queen Victoria, who wore it during the period of mourning for Prince Albert. Jet is fossilised wood which turns from its natural brown colour to the deepest black ('jet-black', as we say) once it is polished, and Whitby proved a particularly fruitful site. This craft trade expanded as women took the royal lead and took to wearing jet ornaments. But their tastes were too fickle for the business to last, and by the time of Victoria's death the demand for Whitby jet was much reduced. Today you can find original pieces of jewellery displayed in Whitby's Pannett Park Museum, and for sale in the town's antiques shops. Some new jet jewellery is being made too.

The abbey ruins dominate part of the town and are a splendid coastal landmark, opposite

undertake whaling expeditions, using the sturdy ships already being built here. They spent many weeks at sea in the distant waters of the Arctic. The trade was lucrative for those who survived; some ships, sadly, never returned. Records reveal that almost 3,000 whales were brought back to Whitby up to 1833. Seals, walruses and polar bears also featured in these hauls, and even unicorns, if the records are to be believed. They were more likely to have been narwhals, whose single 'horn' probably started the unicorn myth in the first place.

The whale blubber was rendered down on the quayside to make oil; the stench, by all accounts, was vile. Even the streetlamps of the town were lit with gas refined from whale oil. An arch formed from the jawbone of a whale looks down upon the harbour today.

Smaller boats sailed out of Whitby to net herring, and the fish market was one of the busiest. The men still fish, but on a much reduced scale; many of the boats that slip anchor today are carrying sea anglers and other visitors.

The town has a special place in ecclesiastical history. In the year AD 655 King Oswy of Northumbria celebrated a victory in battle by promising his daughter as a bride of Christ. He founded a monastery on Whitby's eastern cliff, overlooking the town, much where the later abbey's ruins still stand today. The first abbess was Hilda, who presided over a community of nuns and monks. Her goodness and piety passed into legend, and she was recognised as a saint. It was here, in 664, that the Synod of Whitby convened to decide whether Northumbria should follow Catholic or Celtic Christianity. In the event the Catholic Church triumphed.

The most notable member of this early monastic community was Caedmon, known as the 'Father of English poetry'. A shy man, he preferred to keep his own company as a cowherd instead of singing with the choir. Brother Caedmon had a dream in which an angel asked him to sing. On awakening he found he was possessed of a beautiful voice. His poem, *The Song of Creation*, is the earliest known poem in English. A sandstone cross commemorating Caedmon stands by St Mary's Church; carved panels illustrate some of the incidents in his life.

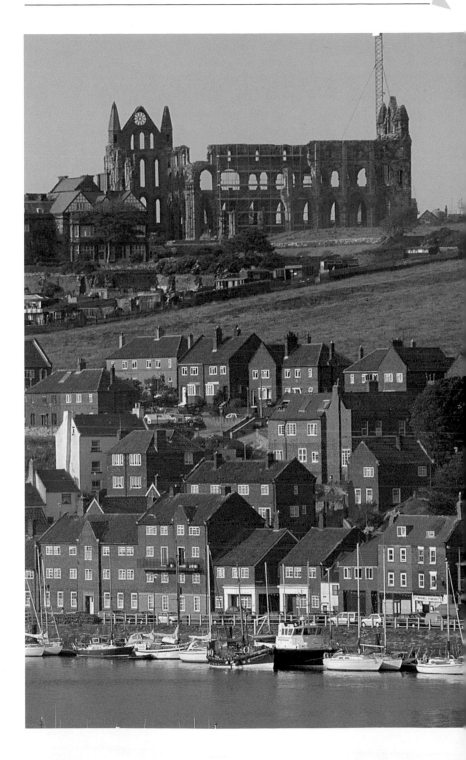

DRACULA

Few graveyards enjoy a more panoramic view than the one surrounding St Mary's Church. But if the wind is whipping around the gravestones, and the full moon is shrouded by clouds, it can have a rather more menacing air. Bram Stoker recognised its potential and readers of his novel, *Dracula*, will recognise some of the settings as Whitby. Look out for the skull and crossbones gravestones near the topmost gate. These are said to have inspired the novel.

Jet, so fashionable as mourning jewellery in Victorian times, is still carved in Whitby today

St Hilda's original abbey was destroyed by Viking raiders. The abbey that replaced it was begun in the 11th century and rebuilt on several occasions, notably in the 13th and 14th centuries; this is what we can see today, starkly silhouetted against the sky. This building, too, suffered damage. In 1914 two German battleships shelled the town and inadvertently hit the west front of Whitby Abbey.

Sharing the abbey's windswept site is St Mary's Church, built to cater for the spiritual needs of the village that grew up around the abbey. St Mary's still serves the needs of congregations today, though parishioners have to tackle the famous 199 steps up to the church. Parts of the building date back to the 12th century; fortunately the fabric of the church suffered none of the indignities meted out to the abbey.

Make sure to take a look inside; the interior was fitted out during the 18th century with wooden galleries, high-sided box-pews and a splendid three-decker pulpit. The effect is startling, with a distinctly nautical feeling as the craftsmen were more accustomed to fitting out ships.

At the bottom of Church Steps is the oldest part of town. Fishermen's cottages huddle together as if to keep out bitter weather. Narrow alleyways lead off from the diminutive market square, and if those 199 steps have taken their toll enjoy a drink in one of the harbour-side pubs and watch the fishing boats and pleasure craft.

On Grape Lane you will find the home of ship owner and Quaker, Captain John Walker, to whom the young James Cook was apprenticed before enlisting in the Royal Navy. Today the building houses the Captain Cook Memorial Museum, with room sets and exhibits about his life.

Esk Dale and the North

Leisure Information
Places of Interest
Shopping
The Performing Arts
Sports, Activities and the Outdoors
Annual Events and Customs

Checklist ✓

Leisure Information

TOURIST INFORMATION CENTRES

Danby
The Moors Centre. Tel: 01287 660654.
Great Ayton
High Green Car Park. Tel: 01642 722835 (Seasonal).
Guisborough
Priory Grounds, Church Street. Tel: 01287 633801.
Whitby
Langborne Road. Tel: 01947 602674.

OTHER INFORMATION

English Heritage (Yorkshire Region)
37 Tanner Row, York. Tel: 01904 601901.
www.english-heritage.org.uk
Environment Agency
Rivers House, 21 Park Square South, Leeds. Tel: 0113 2440191.
Forest Enterprise
Outgang Road, Pickering. Tel: 01751 472771.
Moorsbus summer coach and minibus
Tel: 01439 770657.
www.moorsbus.net
National Trust
Goddards, 27 Tadcaster Road,
York. Tel: 01904 702021.
www.nationaltrust.org.uk
North York Moors National Park
The Old Vicarage, Bondgate, Helmsley. Tel: 01439 770657.
www.northyorkmoors-npa.gov.uk
Useful Websites
www.north-york-moors.com
www.yorkshirenet.co.uk
www.york-moors.co.uk
Yorkshire Tourist Board
312 Tadcaster Road, York. Tel: 01904 707961.
www.ytb.org.uk
Yorkshire Wildlife Trust
10 Toft Green, York. Tel: 01904 659570. www.yorkshire-wildlife-trust.org.uk

ORDNANCE SURVEY MAPS

Landranger 1:50,000. Sheets 93, 94.

Places of Interest

There will be an admission charge at the following places of interest unless otherwise stated.
Captain Cook and Staithes Heritage Centre
High Street, Staithes. Tel: 01947 841454. Open daily; weekends only in Jan.
Captain Cook Memorial Museum
Grape Lane, Whitby. Tel: 01947 601900. Open Apr–Oct daily (afternoons only); Aug all day.
Captain Cook Schoolroom Museum
Great Ayton. Tel: 01642 724296. Open afternoons Apr–Oct (Jul & Aug 11–4).
The Dracula Experience
9 Marine Parade, Whitby. Tel: 01947 601923. Open Easter–Sep daily; Oct–Easter

Steaming ahead at Grosmont

weekends only.

Gisborough Priory
Guisborough. Tel: 01287
638301. Open Apr–Sep,
Tue–Sun; Oct–Mar, Wed–Sun.

Lifeboat Museum
Pier Road, Whitby. Tel: 01947
606094. Open Easter–Oct, daily.
Free.

**Museum of Victorian
Whitby**
4 Sandgate, Whitby. Tel: 01947
601221. Open daily.

The Moors Centre
Lodge Lane, Danby. Tel: 01287
660654. Open daily.

Tocketts Watermill
On A173, 1 mile (1.6km) east of
Guisborough. Tel: 01287
634437. Open Sun afternoons in
summer only.

**Tom Leonard Mining
Museum**
Skinningrove. Tel: 01287
642877. Open Apr–Oct, daily;
afternoons only.

Victorian Jet Works
123B Church Street, Whitby.
Tel: 01947 821530. Open all
year daily. Shop free; fee for
museum.

Whitby Abbey
East Cliff, Whitby.
Tel: 01947 603568. Open all
year daily.

**Whitby Museum and Art
Gallery**
Pannett Park, Whitby.
Tel: 01947 602908. Open all
year daily (closed Mon
Oct–Apr).

Shopping

Guisborough
Open-air market, Thu and Sat.
Whitby
Open-air market, Sat.

LOCAL SPECIALITIES

**Ceramics, Sculpture and
Jewellery**
Montage Studio Gallery, 12
Church Street, Castleton.
Tel: 01287 660159.

Enamel
The Enamel Gallery, 128 Church
Street. Whitby.

Glass
Whitby Glass Studios, 9
Sandgate, Whitby. Tel: 01947
603553.

Paintings and Prints
John Freeman Studios, 8 Market
Place, Whitby. Tel: 01947
602799.
Grosmont Gallery, Grosmont.
Tel: 01947 895007.

Whitby Jet
Watsons Jet Workshop, 151
Church Street, Whitby. Tel:
01947 605320.
Victorian Jet Works, Church
Street, Whitby. Tel: 01947
821530. Open all year, daily.
Shop free; fee for workshop.

The Performing Arts

Whitby Pavilion Theatre
West Cliff, Whitby. Tel: 01947
604455.

Sports, Activities and the Outdoors

ANGLING

Sea
Staithes & Whitby
Enquire at the harbour, or
contact local Tourist Information
Centre.

Fly
River Esk
Information on licences and
permits from main post offices.
Details of fishing locations from
the Environment Agency, Rivers
House, 21 Park Square South,
Leeds. Tel: 0113 2440191.
Scaling Dam Reservoir
Tel: 01287 640540. Permits
from coin-operated machine on
site.

BEACHES

Runswick Bay has a sandy beach
with easy access; a sandy beach
stretches from Whitby to
Sandsend with car parks and
access points.

BOAT TRIPS

Whitby
Trips to Runswick Bay and Robin
Hood's Bay leave from the
Bandstand, West Pier.

CYCLE HIRE

Castleton
Trailways Cycle Hire,
The Old Railway Station,
Hawsker, nr Whitby. Tel: 01947
820207.

GOLF COURSE

Whitby
Whitby Golf Club, Sandsend
Road, Low Straggleton.
Tel: 01947 602719.

HORSE-RIDING

Lealholm
Hollin Hall Riding Centre, Great
Fryup Dale. Tel: 01947 897470.
Staithes
Borrowby Equestrian Centre,
High Farm, Borrowby.
Tel: 01947 840134.

LONG-DISTANCE
FOOTPATHS AND TRAILS

The Cleveland Way
A 110-mile (176-km) walk from
Helmsley to Filey Brigg.
www.clevelandway.gov.uk
The Esk Valley Walk
Begins at Castleton and follows
the River Esk to Whitby.

WATERSPORTS

Scaling Reservoir
Tel: 01287 634383. Sailing,
windsurfing.

Annual Events and Customs

Castleton
Castleton Show, late August.
Danby
Agricultural Show, mid-August.
Egton
Egton Show, late August.
Egton Bridge
Gooseberry Show, early August.
Kildale
Kildale Show, early September.
Lealholm
Lealholm Show, early
September.
Whitby
Planting of the Penny Hedge,
Ascension Eve, May.
Whitby Festival, June.
Blessing of Boats, mid-July.
Whitby Angling Festival, July.
Whitby Folk Festival, August.
Whitby Regatta, mid-August.

The checklists give details of just
some of the facilities within the
area covered by this guide.
Further information can be
obtained from Tourist
Information Centres.

The Western Moors

The Western Moors include Helmsley, a handsome little market town and the administrative centre of the National Park – this is a good base from which to explore the area. Near by are the White Horse of Kilburn and the ruins of Rievaulx Abbey. St Aelred, third abbot of Rievaulx, wrote more than eight centuries ago 'Everywhere peace, everywhere serenity, and a marvellous freedom from the tumult of the world'. The typical landscape is one of heather moorland and pastoral dales, dotted with isolated farmhouses and villages of stone houses with red-tiled roofs. The freedom of the moors is something to be cherished; here, even at the busiest of times, you will find room to roam.

AMPLEFORTH Map ref SE5878

Best known for its boys' public school and Benedictine Monastery, Ampleforth is a linear village of handsome houses overlooking the Howardian Hills. The Benedictine Abbey was not destroyed by Henry VIII's Dissolution of the Monasteries for the simple reason that it was founded many years after that event.

French monks, having fled their homeland in 1793 to escape persecution during the French Revolution, found sanctuary in England and patronage from the prominent Fairfax family settling at Ampleforth in 1802. Theirs had been a teaching order, so they continued their calling by

Ampleforth College, one of England's foremost Roman Catholic public schools

AMPLEFORTH COLLEGE

Founded by Benedictine monks who fled from France, the school opened its doors in 1802. The first intake, under the headmastership of Father Bolton, was a mere two pupils, but the school prospered from these small beginnings to become one of the most eminent Roman Catholic schools in the country.

building a school within the monastery. The oldest surviving school buildings date to 1861, the monastery buildings to 1894–8. But both establishments have been extended almost continuously up to the present day.

Just after the end of World War I, headmaster Father Paul Nevill, who was also the parish priest, commissioned Robert Thompson of Kilburn (see page 64) to make a wooden cross for the churchyard in the village. Thompson's reputation had not yet spread afar, but Father Nevill was so impressed by the woodcarver's craftsmanship that Thompson was asked to make furniture for the school. The library remains one of Thompson's most ambitious commissions. The present abbey church is a new addition, built between 1922 and 1961 to a design by Sir Gilbert Scott; it too contains woodwork and carvings by Robert Thompson.

South-east of Ampleforth is Gilling East which has a 14th-century fortified tower house. For most of this century the building has been owned by Ampleforth College, and used as the college's preparatory school. The gardens are open to the public and the Elizabethan Great Chamber may sometimes be seen on application.

BILSDALE

The long valley of Bilsdale extends along the B1257, from Helmsley in the south towards Stokesley in the north. The broad valley is farmed up to the moorland tops, as it was, centuries ago, by the monks of Rievaulx Abbey. The monastic connection is recalled by names such as Crossholme and Low Crosses Farm. Scattered farms punctuate the valley, but today the only village – and a tiny one at that – is Chop Gate. Pronounce it as 'Chop Yat' if you want to sound like a local.

Verdant Bilsdale provides rich pastureland below the moors

The original Sun Inn sports an unusual cruck frame

Bilsdale's name is one to baffle the local historians. A hoary old tale relates that during the Harrying of the North, William the Conqueror marched his troops through Bilsdale on his way to York. Getting lost in a typical moorland mist, he lost contact with his men. His intemperate language was the origin of the phrase 'to swear like Billy-O'. It is, however, a little ingenuous to conclude that Bilsdale means 'Bill's Dale', especially as an older name is 'Dildes Dale' and probably refers to the rocky outcrops which can be found towards the head of the valley.

The River Seph is ever-present in the valley bottom; the B1257 accompanies it almost from its source to where it joins the River Rye to the north of Rievaulx. Don't hurry past the Sun Inn, situated on the roadside about 8 miles (12.8km) north of Helmsley. For the last 200 years there has been no need to change the licensee's name above the door; that's as long as the landlord has been a William Ainsley. Just yards from the pub is a much earlier thatched building, of cruck-frame construction, that dates back to the 16th century. This was the original Sun Inn – also known as Spout House – which was dispensing ale from first receiving its licence in 1714 until 1914.

When the licence transferred to the new Sun Inn, the older building fell into disrepair. Fortunately, the National Park Authority rescued and renovated this delightful example of vernacular architecture. Now it is the finest example of a cruck-framed house to be found in the National Park (not counting those in the Ryedale Folk Museum) and one of the oldest. Once again the sign of the Sun Inn hangs on the wall and a fringe of thatch hangs low over the mullioned windows. Visitors can take a look inside.

The interior has been restored to how it might have looked more than three centuries ago. A witch post still stands near the inglenook fireplace, to ward off the 'evil eye'. Up narrow stairs are tiny rooms, open to the thatch and fitted out with wooden box beds. Downstairs are the equally diminutive bar and snugs of the original pub layout, and the beer cellar.

PICNIC SITES
Five miles (8km) north of Helmsley on the B1257, just before you enter Bilsdale, is Newgate Bank, a fine vantage point with a picnic site, from where you can enjoy views of Bilsdale and the Hambleton Hills. A footpath returns to Helmsley via Riccal Bank. At the northern end of Bilsdale is the village of Chop Gate, which also has a picnic site and a car park.

BRIDESTONES
On top of Hasty Bank, the northern escarpment of the Cleveland Hills, are the Wainstones, the largest outcrop of rocks within the National Park, and a favourite with climbers. Another set of rocks can be found on Nab End Moor, in Bilsdale. These are just one of a number of rock formations on the moors that are known as the Bridestones. Others, the remains of ancient stone circles, can be found near Grosmont. But the best-known Bridestones are in the hands of the National Trust on Bridestones Moor, and are most easily approached from the Dalby Forest Drive. This collection of rocks, weathered into strange shapes, makes a surreal moorland landmark.

THE GILLAMOOR SUNDIAL

Gillamoor boasts a sundial of novel design in front of Dial House Farm; it was erected by public subscription in 1800. A central column is mounted on top of a stepped base. On top is a stone globe mounted on an inscribed cube, with a dial face on four of its sides.

BRANSDALE

The unspoiled valley of Bransdale drives deep into the moors, but most visitors pass it by. Motorists leaving Helmsley along the main A170 towards Kirkbymoorside should look out on the left for a signpost to Carlton (and Helmsley Youth Hostel). A glance at the map reveals that the road loops around Bransdale and returns to the A170 about 5 miles (8km) further east at Kirkbymoorside. No matter; it's a delightful drive.

Beyond the knot of houses comprising the village of Carlton, the views open up dramatically. To the left is unenclosed heather moorland; to the right the valley bottom is divided up by neat drystone walls either side of Hodge Beck. This pattern is punctuated by a handful of scattered farmsteads. Their unfussy designs, of well-dressed, honey-coloured stone, harmonise perfectly with an almost timeless landscape. The moors, with barely a tree to be seen, echo to the evocative calls of the curlew, red grouse and lapwing; sheep graze the grassy verges and wander idly across the road.

The road, unenclosed for most of the way, heads north; look out on the left for examples of crudely inscribed milestones. At the head of the valley is Cockayne, a village in name only, but what a name. The land of Cockayne is, according to legend, a mythical place of indolence and luxury, though Bransdale's tiny community probably derives its name, more prosaically, from 'kirk', a church.

The Church of St Nicholas sits on a hillock overlooking the valley. Though dating only from 1886, the present building replaces a much earlier church. It is a typical moorland church, tiny and undemonstrative, but with a sense of spirituality that larger, more self-important churches so often lack. Inside, the barrelled roof is worth a look.

Flour was ground for centuries at Bransdale Mill (National Trust, not open to the public), accessible, on foot only, from either side of the valley head. The present building, dating from 1811, was built by William Strickland and his son, Emmanuel, vicar of Ingleby Greenhow. Stones, inset into the mill walls, are inscribed with 'improving' texts in Hebrew, Latin and Greek; evidence of the vicar's classical education.

The road makes a broad sweep to the right, before continuing the circuit of Bransdale. Sturdy farmsteads with fanciful names – Cow Sike, Toad Hole and Spout House – gaze down into the valley. Before arriving in Kirkbymoorside, you have a chance to visit Gillamoor and Fadmoor, a pair of typical moorland villages barely half a mile (800m) apart.

The houses of both villages are grouped around a village green, but Gillamoor has an extra surprise in store. The church stands on its own at the end of the village; you are almost upon it before you see that it is sited on the edge of a steep precipice which commands breathtaking views across lower Farndale, the River Dove and to the heather moors beyond.

A CYCLE TOUR THROUGH BRANSDALE

The unclassified road which leaves the A170 at Helmsley and curves round in a loop through Bransdale before rejoining the A170 again at Kirkbymoorside is an ideal tour for cyclists. Passing through the villages of Carlton, Cockayne and Gillamoor the 12-mile (19-km) route offers wonderful moorland views with lonely farms and tumbling streams.

An old milestone on the moors marks the road to Helmsley

The communities of the North York Moors were well served with churches and chapels

ANCIENT WAYMARKERS
More than 30 moorland crosses still survive today; at one time there were many more. One of their functions was to define the boundaries of the sheep-grazing moors of the monasteries. But their religious symbolism is obvious, and many a lost and lonely traveller would have had his spirits lifted by the sight of a cross on the horizon. Crosses were sited along old roads; many doubled as waymarkers. An interesting custom was for well-heeled travellers to leave coins on top of the crosses (many had a recess for this purpose) for the benefit of their needier brethren.

CHRISTIANITY ON THE MOORS

The life and landscape of the North York Moors have been shaped by many influences; few have had a longer or more profound effect than the Christian faith. The moorland monasteries may be evocative ruins today, but in the past the influence of these communities extended far beyond the silence of their cloisters. By the 16th century, for example, about a third of the land within what is now the National Park was under the direct control of the monasteries.

The monks combined their religious devotions with remarkably successful forays into more secular activities. They may have chosen isolated sites on which to build their churches and communities, but they were not averse to comfort – even luxury. The religious buildings of the moors trace their origins back many centuries. A number of extant churches and abbeys pre-date the Norman invasion. Many more recent edifices are built on the foundations of much earlier buildings. The link with the past is everywhere to be seen.

At the dawning of the 7th century, the moors formed part of the Northumbrian Kingdom of Deira. King Edwin of Northumbria was saved from assassination by the intervention of Lilla, one of his ministers. Edwin is said to have marked Lilla's grave on Fylingdales Moor with a stone cross – the oldest of the famous moorland crosses. Edwin was converted to Christianity by Paulinus, a Roman missionary, in AD 627. The first Christian communities in the area covered by this book were situated in Whitby (at that time known as Streanaeshalch) and Lastingham. In AD 654 St Cedd was given land at Lastingham on which to build a monastery. Three years later Whitby Abbey was founded by Abbess Hilda, who presided over both male and female devotees on this exposed cliff-top site.

Although the monasteries of both Whitby and Lastingham were sacked by the Vikings, the seeds of Christianity proved to have been sown in fertile ground. By the end of the 10th century the Danish and Norwegian settlers had themselves mostly been converted to the faith. St Gregory's Minster at Kirkdale is a fascinating example of a pre-Norman church.

It was only after the Norman invasion, however, that the great monastic houses on the moors were founded. Benedictine monks returned to the site of St Hilda's Celtic monastery in Whitby and established another five communities in the area. The Cistercian Order was created by French monks. Finding the Benedictine regime too ready to succumb to earthly temptations, they vowed to emphasise once again the virtues of hard work and austerity. In 1131 a band of monks from France crossed the Channel and were endowed with land in Ryedale on which to build a monastery. The monks gave a French twist to the valley's name and called their community Rievaulx.

From small beginnings the Cistercian community prospered. By the time of the third abbot, St Aelred, the number of ordained monks – about 150 – was swelled by more than 600 lay brethren. Outlying farms, known as 'granges', were set up – often at some distance from the mother church. Contemplation and prayer certainly played a great part in the monks' lives, but they worked hard too.

The monks of Rievaulx developed the mining of ironstone that, many centuries on, would help to create the industrial wealth around the Tees and the Tyne. The

'PAGANS PLAY WHERE GOD WAS PRAISED'

Danish invaders sacked many of these northern communities on the moors. Alcuin, an Anglo-Saxon monk, wrote feelingly of the Viking raids:

'Never before has such an atrocity been seen in Britain as we have now suffered at the hands of a pagan people... Pagans play where God was praised'.

In 657 King Oswy gave his daughter, Hilda, land to found a monastery after he was successful in battle against a pagan king. Whitby Abbey was the result

ENTREPRENEURIAL MONKS
The monastic communities of the moors owned outlying farms – known as granges – which were often located many miles from the monasteries. The monks (their numbers augmented by lay brothers) devoted their talents to arable farming, animal husbandry and exploiting the uplands for their mineral wealth. The monks' entrepreneurial skills created international markets for their wares and, in many cases, immense wealth for the monasteries.

Rievaulx Abbey was one of the great monastic houses of the north

upland moors provided grazing for huge flocks of sheep. The land (a gift from a local landowner) may have been poor for agriculture, but the monks successfully exploited it as grazing land. Wool from Rievaulx became renowned throughout Europe for its excellence.

The monks cleared forests to provide fuel for the iron furnaces. They drained land, built roads and spanned the Rye and other rivers with sturdy bridges. They even built a system of canals to facilitate the transport of iron and building stone. All this activity was in addition to the huge task, undertaken over a period of 60 years, of building Rievaulx Abbey itself; the impressive remains of the high church and monastic buildings still inspire visitors today.

The Carthusian Order was another to have had its origins in France. Mount Grace Priory, near Osmotherley, was founded in 1398; the ruins are the finest example of Carthusian building in the country.

Franciscan friars, following the teachings of St Francis, came to Scarborough. Their strict doctrine of absolute poverty must have provided a stark contrast to the business-like ethos of the Carthusians. The Augustinian Canons built Gisborough Priory; the great arch of the east window still stands today.

Between 1536 and 1540, after his break with Rome, Henry VIII ordered the closure of the abbeys and monasteries, bringing to an end their huge and wide-ranging influence.

The Cleveland Way long-distance footpath starts at Helmsley

THE CLEVELAND WAY

When it was inaugurated in 1969 the Cleveland Way was only the second national trail in the country – coming just four years after Tom Stephenson's pioneering work in creating the Pennine Way. The name of the walk is a little ambiguous, since for most of its 110-mile (176-km) length it lies inside the North York Moors National Park making only a brief foray into what is now the county of Cleveland. The name of the walk actually derives from the Cleveland Hills.

The walk, a roughly horseshoe-shaped route, breaks into two distinct and contrasting sections. From the starting point at Helmsley, the route meanders through the moorland scenery of the Hambleton and Cleveland Hills. Walkers reach the highest point within the National Park when they traverse Urra Moor. Once the North Sea is sighted, at Saltburn, walkers follow the coastal path down to the finishing point at Filey Brigg.

The walk can further be divided up into sections that offer a single day's hike, with each section ending at a point where budget accommodation is available. Of course, for every walker who tackles the Cleveland Way in one go, there are probably hundreds who opt to avoid the blisters by walking it in easy stages.

THE MISSING LINK

An extra section of the Cleveland Way, known as the Missing Link, has been created to take walkers in a complete loop from Scarborough back to Helmsley. This circular walk is about 180 miles (288km) long, and means that walkers can now start and finish at any convenient point on the route.

Discover the Western Moors

A 60-mile (88.5-km) tour through the western moors and dales, around the Cleveland and Hambleton Hills and taking in Rievaulx Abbey, Byland Abbey, Coxwold and Helmsley along the way. The best walking is around Chop Gate in Bilsdale, and Sutton Bank. A section of the tour is on narrow roads; please drive with care. The tour begins at Helmsley, the National Park's administrative centre, and a handsome little town in its own right.

ROUTE DIRECTIONS

See Key to Car Tours on page 122.

Begin the drive in Helmsley along the B1257, signposted 'Stokesley'. After 2 miles (3.2km), turn left down an unclassified road, signed 'Old Byland'. Bear right immediately before a little bridge, over the River Rye, to see the impressive ruins of **Rievaulx Abbey** ahead, in a delightful setting.

The route passes through the village of Rievaulx

Drive past the abbey, through Rievaulx village and sharply uphill to rejoin the B1257. Turn left, signed 'Stokesley'. As you pass a conifer forest on your right, beautiful views open up of Bilsdale ahead. Drive through the scattered houses of Chop Gate. As you top Hasty Bank with its viewpoint look out on the right for the distinctive profile of Roseberry Topping.

At Great Broughton turn left, signed 'Kirkby' and 'Carlton', with the escarpment of the Cleveland Hills rearing up on your left. Go right at the T-junction, then left, on to the main A172 in the direction of Thirsk. After 2½ miles (3.4km) turn left, signed 'Swainby'. Cross the bridge in Swainby, a pleasant village astride a beck, and bear immediately left. Climb gradually uphill on to Scarth Wood Moor. Pass Cod Beck Reservoir and continue on into Osmotherley.

Bear right, in the centre of the village, by the market cross and intriguing stone 'table'; the signs are for Northallerton and Thirsk. Turn right again at the T-junction on to the A19, signed 'Thirsk,' to join the dual carriageway southbound. Leave at the second turning on the left, signed 'Over Silton'. For the next few miles you are on narrow, unclassified roads, so drive with care. Drive through Over Silton to a T-junction; go left, signed 'Kepwick and Cowesby'. Enjoy beautiful views over farmland to the moor tops beyond. Drive uphill to a T-junction, adjacent to the gatehouse of Kepwick Hall; go right here, through the pleasant little village of Kepwick. Take the next turning on the left, signed 'Cowesby'. Drive through Cowesby to the village of Kirby Knowle. Pass the parish church and turn left towards Felixkirk. Take the next two left turns, both signed 'Boltby'.

Descend into Boltby, a happy arrangement of cottages in the honey-coloured stone so typical of this area. Climb steeply out of the village, through Boltby Forest; after a second steep section the road levels out. Turn right, signed 'Old Byland and Cold Kirby'. Follow this ruler-straight section, it is part of the old Hambleton Drove Road – as you turn right you can see the old, unmetalled track continuing to the left. At the end turn right at a T-junction, signed 'Thirsk and Sutton Bank'. Pass the car park at the top of Sutton Bank. If you need to stretch your legs, this is the ideal spot – a waymarked path along the top of the bank offers easy walking and breathtaking views across the Vale of York and beyond.

Go left at a T-junction by the car park, on to the A170, signed 'Scarborough'. Take the first turning on the right, signed 'White Horse Bank'. Pass a flying club and drive downhill through woodland to the White Horse car park. A short walk from here allows a closer investigation of the famous white horse, carved into the steep hillside in 1857 – though, in truth, this is one landmark that looks better from a distance.

Continue down to a T-junction; turn right to drive into the village of Kilburn. Look out for a half-timbered building: the furniture making workshops and showroom founded by craftsman Robert Thompson.

Drive through the village; go left at a T-junction to arrive in the main street of Coxwold. Laurence Sterne (author of *The Life and Opinions of Tristram Shandy, Gentleman*) was once vicar here. Opposite the church is his home, Shandy Hall, which is now a museum devoted to the novelist's life and work. Turn left at the crossroads at the bottom of the village, signed 'Byland Abbey and Helmsley'.

Pass the evocative ruins of **Byland Abbey**, drive through Wass and on to Ampleforth then pass Ampleforth Abbey with its famous public school. Oswaldkirk is next; at the end of the village bear left, steeply uphill, signed 'Helmsley'. At the top of the hill turn left, along the B1257 and left

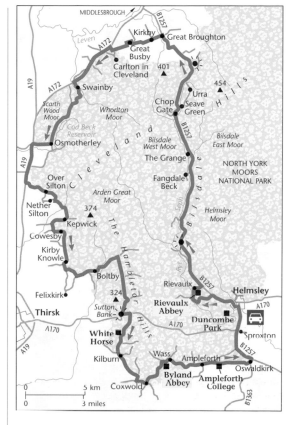

again at the Trafalgar Arch at Sproxton soon return to Helmsley and the start of the tour.

Look out for the strange green telephone box by Fangdale Beck, Bilsdale

The delightfully rambling Shandy Hall reflects the life of its most famous inhabitant, Laurence Sterne

COXWOLD   Map ref SE5377

It's a fair bet that more people know of Laurence Sterne than have ever read his books. Nevertheless, *Tristram Shandy* is indisputably one of the comic classics of English literature, and the Reverend Sterne remains one of the novel's more eccentric practitioners. Born in southern Ireland in 1713, Sterne's early years were marred first by the death of his father and then by being disowned by his mother. After graduating from Cambridge he took holy orders.

As a writer Sterne was a late developer, not picking up his quill pen until the age of 46. The publication of his picaresque novel, *The Life and Opinions of Tristram Shandy, Gentleman*, coincided with him becoming the vicar of Coxwold. Literary success was immediate, and Sterne was able to indulge his taste for high living.

His 15th-century house opposite the village church was renamed Shandy Hall, and here Sterne lived the life of a literary gentleman. While preparing for the publication of *A Sentimental Journey through France and Italy*, in 1768, Sterne contracted pleurisy and died. He is buried in Coxwold churchyard. Dilapidated Shandy Hall was rescued in the 1960s by the Laurence Sterne Trust, then renovated and filled with manuscripts and first editions and opened to the public.

The village church, with its distinctive eight-sided tower, overlooks the handsome houses lining the broad main street of the village, which include almshouses dating back to the reign of Charles II.

Immediately to the south of Coxwold is Newburgh Priory, built in 1145 as an Augustinian house. After the

MARY FAUCONBERG

Oliver Cromwell's daughter, Mary Fauconberg, lived at Newburgh Priory from 1647 to 1700. A story relates that she managed to take her father's head down from the gallows at Tyburn, and to bury it secretly in the attic of the porch of Newburgh Priory. It is said that another head was put in his place. Certainly there are a number of Cromwellian relics – including his saddle and pistol – that can still be seen today.

Dissolution of the Monasteries, Henry VIII rewarded the loyalty of his chaplain, Anthony Bellasis, by giving him the building. He, and the owners who followed him, transformed the priory into a delightful country house.

The beautiful setting of Byland Abbey (English Heritage) was not the first site chosen by the band of Cistercian monks who came here from France. They had settled briefly near Old Byland, which was reckoned unsuitable because the monks were confused by hearing the bells of nearby Rievaulx Abbey. Finally, in 1177, work began on Byland Abbey. Not as complete as either Rievaulx or Fountains Abbeys, its church was nevertheless larger than either.

The dramatic west façade, with its 26-foot (8-m) diameter window, still stands substantially to its full height, and gives a convincing impression of just how huge the nave used to be.

A SPORTING VICAR
Laurence Sterne's spiritual ambitions had to compete with his love of gambling, horse racing and cock fighting. On one occasion, while vicar of Stillington, near York, he left his congregation to amuse themselves while he went after partridges with his shotgun.

The ruined façade of Byland Abbey

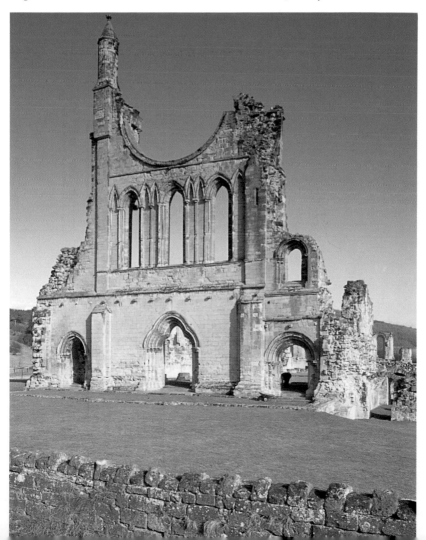

The Hills of Hawnby

A remote village, in one of the loveliest parts of the National Park, provides the half-way point of a walk, full of variety, taking in both Easterside Hill and Hawnby Hill.

Time: 3 hours. Distance: 5 miles (8km).
Location: 10 miles (16.1km) east of Northallerton.
Start: Park at Moor Gate, about 2 miles (3.2km) north of Hawnby village, on the road to Osmotherley. There is plenty of room by the cattle grid. (OS grid ref: SE539917.)
OS Map: Outdoor Leisure 26 (North York Moors – Western area) 1:25,000.
See Key to Walks on page 123.

ROUTE DIRECTIONS

From the parking place there are two tracks that meander east across the moorland. Ignore the track that aims for the Bilsdale TV mast and take the track to the right, with views opening up of the rounded outcrop of Easterside Hill.

It is level walking from here to an isolated farm, called Sportsman's Hall. Go through a gate, but keep left of the farm buildings. Just after a corrugated iron barn, follow the direction of the signed yellow arrows across a field, pass through a gap in the wall and bear immediately right downhill into a copse and on to a wooden footbridge which spans Ladhill Beck.

Bear slightly right uphill, aiming for the top of the wall ahead. Cross a ditch at the top of the wall and take a path ahead through the heather. When you meet a wall, walk left along it. Once you crest the hill, bleak moorland gives way to panoramic views down into Bilsdale. Follow the wall as it bears to the right, to skirt the shoulder of Easterside Hill.

The path follows the 240-metre contour, so the walking is level and easy, with delightful views opening up of lonely farms and wooded hillsides. Eventually the track leads downhill to a stile and then a road. Turn right on to this minor road, which has verges and carries very little traffic; this is your route to **Hawnby**. Hairpin bends provide a steep descent then ascent, both 1-in-3, to reach the village.

Walk through the village of Hawnby, taking the Kepwick road past the Hawnby Hotel – a good place for refreshments and a snack. Opposite Manor Farm take a signed footpath to the right, through a gate. Follow the farm track uphill, enjoying ever wider views of wooded hills. Skirt the bottom of a mixed wood and pass lonely Hill End House. Continue along the track, with fields to the left and bracken to the right, for 200 yards (183m) to reach a wooden gate; ahead is unenclosed moorland and Bilsdale TV mast.

Your way is straight ahead on a path through the heather, around Hawnby Hill. Keep to the right of a small copse of conifers to return to the meeting of tracks, and your car, at Moor Gate.

POINT OF INTEREST

Hawnby
From a distance, the red-roofed houses of Hawnby (see page 62) seem to cling to the rounded contours of Hawnby Hill. The village certainly occupies a

The cottages of the picturesque village of Hawnby cling to the hillside

particularly lovely position, looking out over Rye Dale.

The houses of Hawnby straggle down a steep hill, with the inn enjoying a panoramic view from the top, and the Church of All Saints at the bottom in a more sheltered spot beside the River Rye.

The walk skirts the eastern flank of Easterside Hill

JOHN CARR

Hawnby's river bridge was the work of John Carr. A distinguished Georgian architect, his commissions included Harewood House, in West Yorkshire, home of the Earl and Countess of Harewood, and the Crescent in Buxton, Derbyshire. Bridges, however, were his stock-in-trade.

HAWNBY Map ref SE5489

The remote village of Hawnby is best approached from the south. A long view opens up, with the red-roofed houses of the village appearing to cling to a ledge on the flank of Hawnby Hill. This sunny situation encourages residents to create colourful terraced gardens. To the right are the equally rounded contours of Easterside Hill; the Walk on page 60 offers an undemanding ramble round these hills, both created by glacial meltwaters. The environs of Hawnby comprise one of the loveliest landscapes in the National Park; it is well worth leaving the car and exploring on foot.

Winding roads and tracks offer delightful views at every turn. This gently undulating moorland landscape certainly left an impression on John Wesley, the founder of Methodism, who came to preach here in 1757: 'I rode through one of the pleasantest parts of England to Hawnby'. His preaching must have found willing ears, as Hawnby gained a reputation as a stronghold of Methodism.

He had come from Osmotherley, across the expanse of Snilesworth Moor, so it would have been a great relief to arrive in the sheltered, wooded valley of the River Rye. The road between Hawnby and Osmotherley has a rather better surface than in Wesley's day, but it still twists and turns through beautiful countryside.

The little Church of All Saints, in a riverside setting near the bridge, has features which date back to the 12th century. Beyond the church is Arden Hall (not open to the public), almost hidden in the woods. Built on the site of a 12th-century Benedictine nunnery, the hall is the seat of the Earls of Mexborough. All traces of the nunnery have gone, except for a medieval chimney breast that is now inside the Hall. Mary, Queen of Scots stayed here on her long road to imprisonment and the executioner's axe.

Tiny Hawnby is set in one of the loveliest landscapes in the National Park

HELMSLEY   Map ref SE6183

The handsome market town of Helmsley is where the
National Park Authority has its administrative
headquarters. Here too is a well-stocked Tourist
Information Centre, conveniently sited in the extensive
market square, where visitors can browse for books,
brochures and maps.

It may be only the size of a large village, but Helmsley
has the purposeful, bustling, reassuring air of a county
town. It is especially busy on Friday, which is market
day. The old market cross on its stepped base is still in
place, though the square is dominated by a more
elaborate monument, designed by Sir Gilbert Scott to
commemorate the second Lord Feversham.

A number of roads converge on Helmsley; at one time
this was an important halt on stagecoach routes. A
regular service ran to London from the Black Swan Inn,
which still boasts a large wooden swan in place of the
usual inn sign.

These days more adventurous souls arrive with
walking boots, cagoule and rucksack, for Helmsley is the
starting point of the Cleveland Way (see page 55), a
110-mile (176-km) national trail that takes off across the
moors before following the coastal path down to Filey.
Cleveland wayfarers should follow the 'acorn' signs up
Castlegate, to get an excellent view of the castle standing
'head and shoulders' above the little town, before
descending into Rye Dale and the atmospheric ruins of
Rievaulx Abbey.

As is the case with many other North Yorkshire towns,
behind Helmsley's prosperity is a castle and a prominent
family. Of Walter l'Espec's first castle no traces now
remain; the fortification we see today dates back to the

*The small market town of
Helmsley is an ideal base for
exploring the North York
Moors*

DAYS GONE BY
Helmsley was an important
stop on stagecoach routes in
days gone by, and it is easy to
imagine weary passengers
emerging gratefully from
badly sprung coaches to avail
themselves of refreshment at
one of the many coaching
inns that lined the Market
Square. Some of these public
houses are still giving
hospitality to travellers –
though today most of them
arrive by car.

Old houses back on to the stream at Helmsley, with a view to the golden stone of the church tower, opposite

A FASTIDIOUS VICAR

Charles Norris Gray, vicar of Helmsley from 1870 to the onset of World War I, was a doughty fighter for his chosen causes, which included the state of the drains, the dangers of wearing tight corsets and the lack of personal hygiene among the lower orders. Who knows the state to which Helmsley might have degenerated without such a strong hand on the tiller? The vicarage was one of the many buildings whose restoration Gray supervised; today the building is the administrative centre of the National Park.

THE 'MOUSEMAN'

Robert Thompson's signature, a carved mouse, can be found on all his pieces of furniture. But why a mouse? Thompson revealed in a letter that the idea came to him while working on a church screen. In conversation with another woodcarver he had mentioned that he was as poor as a church mouse. It seemed such an appropriate symbol that Thompson immediately adopted it for all his work.

12th century. Robert de Ros was rewarded for his part in the Norman invasion by being given the manor of Helmsley. The de Ros family owned the castle until it was sold to Sir Charles Duncombe. Now it is in the care of English Heritage.

The castle was built for defence rather than show, yet it didn't witness any military action until the Civil War. It was here that the troops of Colonel Jordan Crossland, a loyal supporter of Charles I, were besieged by the Parliamentarian army of Sir Thomas Fairfax, which numbered a thousand troops. The siege, against what was regarded as one of the country's most impregnable fortresses, lasted three months. It might have lasted longer, but Royalist reinforcements were intercepted, and vital provisions confiscated. Crossland, forced to surrender, marched out of the castle on 22 November 1644, 'with colours flying and drums beating'.

While the Parliamentarian forces accepted this amicable surrender, they dismantled enough of the castle to ensure that it could never again be used by any side in a conflict. But they failed in their attempts to blow up the Norman castle keep, and the eastern wall still stands to its full height of 97 feet (30m), giving an idea of what an impressive fortification it had been.

The years have been kinder to Duncombe Park, 1 mile (1.6km) southwest of Helmsley off the A170. Pride of place in these 600 tranquil acres goes to the splendid 200-room mansion designed by William Wakefield in 1713 as a family home for the Duncombe family and their descendants, the Fevershams. For 60 years the building was used as a girls' school, but in 1985 the present Lord and Lady Feversham took on the mammoth task of restoring the house and making it a family home once again. Now there is public access to both the house and the landscaped parkland, which boasts a delightful terrace walk, with Ionic and Tuscan temples to lend an air of romance. The temples and terrace were to have been linked by a coach drive, never completed, with the complementary Rievaulx Temple Terrace, also built by the Duncombe family.

KILBURN Map ref SE5179

The village of Kilburn has two claims to fame, both of an artistic nature – the White Horse of Kilburn and woodcarver Robert Thompson.

The White Horse, a hill figure cut into the turf which gazes down from the heights of Roulston Scar, and a landmark for miles around, was created by teacher John Hodgson and his pupils in 1857 (see page 75).

Visitors to Kilburn should not miss the workshops and showrooms of Robert Thompson, a woodcarver and cabinet maker whose fame has travelled far and wide. Mr Thompson was a self-taught craftsman whose skill remained largely unappreciated until he was commissioned by the local vicar to make some furniture

The chalky white horse on Roulston Scar above Kilburn first appeared in 1857

THE INVITING MOORS

About 40 per cent of the national park is heather moorland, comprising the largest expanse in England. To see the moors at their colourful best, a sea of purple, make your visit in late summer when the heather is in bloom. The hardy, black-faced Swaledale sheep are at home on the tops, and are brought down in to the valleys only at lambing times. Take care as you drive along the moorland ridge and roads, as the sheep have only the most rudimentary road sense and will dash into your path without warning.

for his church. Encouraged by the results Thompson began to specialise in ecclesiastical furniture. Many Yorkshire churches have pews, pulpits and other fixtures made by him. One of the many pleasures of visiting them is to search for examples of the craftsman's unique trademark: a little carved mouse that stands proud from its surroundings. Many examples are to be found in Kilburn's parish church, where a chapel was dedicated to the 'Mouseman' shortly before his death in 1958.

You can find Thompson's handiwork further afield – including York Minster and Westminster Abbey. Even without the mouse motif, you can recognise it by the heavy designs, the dark tones of the oak wood and the rippled effect left by the adze (a heavy hand tool with an arched cutting blade set at a right-angle to the handle). This is furniture made to last not just a lifetime, but many lifetimes.

As the business expanded, Thompson's own half-timbered house became a showroom. Behind the building are more recent workshops, in which a new generation of woodworkers follows in his footsteps. Those who can't afford one of the substantial pieces of furniture can find smaller wooden items for sale, all featuring Thompson's famous mouse. You can see stacks of neatly piled oak planks outside the workshop, being seasoned before they are used. The outbuildings house an interesting small museum and exhibition centre.

A stream meanders through Kilburn, supplying part of its name: unusual, because here a stream is known as a beck rather than a burn. The 'burn' suffix is a clue that the origins of the village are Anglo-Saxon not Viking.

OSMOTHERLEY   Map ref SE4596

This handsome village, on the junction of roads old and
new, is the starting point of a 42-mile (67-km) route
march across the moors to Ravenscar, known as the Lyke
Wake Walk. Every weekend walkers decant from their
cars, don boots and cagoules, and head for the high
ground. The less energetic can stroll around the village;
those who manage to work up an appetite will find
excellent food on offer in the pubs that surround the old
market place.

Next to the stepped market cross is a curious stone
table; market wares were probably displayed here. John
Wesley certainly put it to good use as an open-air pulpit
on the many occasions he preached in the town.

Near Osmotherley is Mount Grace Priory (National
Trust), though motorists need to make an inconvenient
loop on the A19 dual carriageway to reach it. No matter
– this is the best preserved of the nine Carthusian
priories that were built in England. In most European
monasteries the monks lived and worked together. The
Carthusian Order was particularly strict, however; the
monks not only shunned the outside world, they even
avoided contact with each other.

Each monk (there were 24, including the prior) had his
own two-storey cell and walled garden to the back of it.
Serving hatches adjacent to each cell door were
ingeniously angled so that meals could be passed
anonymously to the monks inside. The cells are grouped

LIFE AT MOUNT GRACE PRIORY

The monks of Mount Grace
Priory certainly led solitary
lives, but they enjoyed a good
standard of living. Clean water
was piped to each cell, an
amenity unknown to those in
the outside world, and their
toilets had running water too.

A CHALLENGING WALK

The Lyke Wake Walk takes its
inspiration from the old
'corpse roads' across the
moors, along which the
deceased were carried to
often distant burial grounds.
Lyke means a corpse, as in a
church lich gate; wake is the
party after a funeral. The high-
level walk between
Osmotherley and Ravenscar
was founded in 1955 as a
challenge walk – the challenge
being to complete the 42
miles (67km) within 24 hours.
However, the route has
suffered erosion due to the
pounding of too many
walking boots.

*A pinnacle stands as the
market 'cross' in the centre
of Osmotherley*

THE HAMBLETON DROVE ROAD

The Hambleton Drove Road is a reminder of the days when drovers brought their cattle down from Scotland to sell at the English markets of York, Malton and beyond. This ancient ridgeway, as ruler-straight as a Roman road for much of its length, kept slow-moving cattle away from local herds and its wide verges offered free grazing. Just as importantly, the drovers were able to avoid the tolls charged for using the turnpike roads.

Many sections of the Hambleton Drove Road have been incorporated into our modern road system. The Cleveland Way uses a section of the drove road, and is easily accessed from Osmotherley.

The extensive ruins of Mount Grace Priory are well worth viewing

around the Great Cloister. While many of them rise no higher today than their foundations, one cell was reconstructed and furnished at the turn of the century to show visitors how the monks would have lived their solitary lives.

The Carthusian Order was founded in 1048 by St Bruno of Reims, who took Christ's sojourn in the desert as the highest example for his monks to follow. They lived like hermits to avoid worldly distractions, with most of their day given over to prayer, study and contemplation. This harsh regime included a service in the middle of the night. Despite these privations, or perhaps because of them, the Carthusian Order grew rapidly. As late as 1530 there was a waiting list for men who wished to join the Mount Grace community.

Mount Grace Priory was founded in 1398 by Thomas de Holland, with the agreement of Richard II. The monks were given a great deal of land, which they rented out to tenant farmers. At the height of their wealth the income generated by the monks of Mount Grace was even greater than that of their Cistercian neighbours at Rievaulx Abbey. Yet the very success of the Carthusian communities contributed to their eventual downfall. Henry VIII ordered them to be disbanded, and in 1539 the keys to Mount Grace Priory were handed to his representatives by John Wilson, the last prior.

Visitors now enter the priory through a manor house, built in 1654 on the site of an earlier gatehouse. It houses exhibitions about the priory and the lives of its monks. The best-preserved part of the priory is the old church, whose tower still stands to its full height. Compared with other monasteries, the church is small and simple.

The handsome parish church of St Oswald dates from Norman times

OSWALDKIRK Map ref SE6278

The village of Oswaldkirk is strung out along the road beneath the steep and well-wooded Oswaldkirk Bank, and looks out across the Ampleforth Valley. The community takes its name from St Oswald's parish church. St Oswald became King of Northumbria at the age of 30 in AD 634 , and has a special place in the history of the Christian Church. What we know about St Oswald comes largely from the *Ecclesiastical History of the English People* written by the Venerable Bede in AD 731.

Oswald was deeply impressed by the monastic community on Iona, founded by St Columba. Once converted to Christianity he grafted the new faith on to familiar customs – for example, building Christian churches on sites of pagan worship. It was Oswald who gave the island of Lindisfarne to St Aidan and the monks of Iona as another sanctuary from which the Christian gospels might be spread.

One Easter, while Oswald and Aidan were about to share a meal, Oswald learned that there was not enough food to feed the poor at the gate. The king gave them his own food, still on its silver platter. Aidan was so moved by this act that he took the king's right hand and said 'May this hand never perish'.

Oswald's faith could not save him from defeat in battle, however. He died in AD 642 while fighting the heathen King Penda of Mercia. Victorious Penda had Oswald's body dismembered and the pieces stuck on stakes. But, as prophesied, Oswald's right hand did not wither, and it was taken to Lindisfarne by Oswald's brother, Oswy, as a venerated relic. Thus began a cult, with Oswald being elevated to sainthood, and tales of miraculous cures being associated with Oswald's bones.

The nave of St Oswald's church is largely Norman; cross fragments confirm that Oswaldkirk was already settled in Anglo-Saxon times. A couple of 'mother and child' sculptures in the porch offer an evocative contrast – one is modern, the other is Anglo-Saxon. Unusually, most of the rectors of Oswaldkirk are known by name; this practice started at the beginning of the 14th century and continues today.

RELIGIOUS RELICS

St Oswald's reputation, and his relics which had gained a reputation for miraculous cures, spread throughout Europe. During the Middle Ages the hawking of religious relics was a lucrative way to make a living and the power of suggestion can, of course, be a powerful medicine.

Old Byland and Rievaulx Abbey

An invigorating ramble around Ryedale, starting from the village of Old Byland, which sits on an exposed plateau above the valley, and taking in a delectable ruin on the way. You could start the walk from Rievaulx, although the car park there is just for visitors to the abbey.

Time: 3 hours. Distance: 6½ miles (10.5km).
Location: 6 miles (9.7km) northeast of Thirsk.
Start: Park in Old Byland village. (OS grid ref: SW550859.)
OS Map: Outdoor Leisure 26 (North York Moors – Western area) 1:25,000.
See Key to Walks on page 123.

ROUTE DIRECTIONS

Leave **Old Byland** by walking downhill on the road, past the green, towards Cold Kirby. About 50 yards (46m) past the Old Byland sign mounted on a millstone, turn left at a gate signed 'Bridleway'. Follow the path downhill into scrubby woodland at the bottom of a shallow valley, then up the opposite side on to a level path. Emerge from the woodland and go through a gate on your right. Walk across the field, and cross the farm track to another gate. Follow the edge of two fields, keeping a hedge to your left, and go through a gate into Callister Wood.

Follow a path to your left, downhill through trees, and cross the beck on a footbridge. Bear left across a little field to a stile, then cross a stony track, go through a gate and over the stepping stones at a picturesque meeting of becks. A signpost indicates that you are joining the Cleveland Way. Bear left after the stepping stones to join the wide track of the Cleveland Way and pass a trio of small lakes on the left.

The track eventually leads to a gate; turn left along a minor road and Ashberry Farm soon comes into view, in a very pleasant site with the beck in front. Ignore the road going left to Old Byland and keep straight ahead to Bridge Cottage, where the beck joins the River Rye. Cross the old stone bridge and bear left along the road towards the village of Rievaulx, with views of magnificent **Rievaulx Abbey** ahead.

After visiting the abbey continue into the village of Rievaulx and look for the sign 'Footpath to Bow Bridge' on the left by a stable block. Go through gates in quick succession to take a field path ahead. The water-filled dyke to your right was one of the monks' canals. Meet the River Rye and cross a pair of stiles. Continue with the river on your left, then take a stile on your right to join a track that leads down to the graceful stone arch of Bow Bridge. Cross the bridge and continue along the track for 110 yards (101m), before turning right through a gate with a footpath signed 'Hawnby'. Follow the fence to approach the river once again. After a stile there are duckboards. Walk through woodland, across low-lying pasture, then uphill to a stile and tarmac farm track.

Go right, uphill, along the track. Lovely views open up behind you, as you approach solitary Tylas Farm. Immediately above the farm, bear sharp left up another track; the views over Rye Dale compensate for the steep climb. Keep left of a barn complex to follow the well-defined edge of deeply

wooded Oxen Dale. Where the valley abruptly ends, leave the track by a stile to the right signed 'Old Byland'.

Follow the path along field edges; at the far side of the fourth field a sign directs you to the left. Two fields later negotiate a stile and come out on to a road. Go right to return to Old Byland.

POINTS OF INTEREST

Old Byland

Cistercian monks travelled to Ryedale from Furness Abbey, in 1143, hoping to found a new community here, but they abandoned the site, which was near Tylas Farm, eventually settling at Byland Abbey. The village of Old Byland

was originally centred on its monastic grange, or dependent farm, and retains its medieval layout around a village green

Rievaulx Abbey

The abbey (see page 72) is a

The walk explores the attractive wooded area around Old Byland and Rievaulx Abbey

spectacular ruin in pale stone at the meeting of two valleys, Rye Dale and Nettle Dale. The compact village of Rievaulx grew up only after the Dissolution of the Monasteries, when stone from the abbey was plundered and used to build many of the pretty cottages, some thatched, that now surround it.

NAMING RIEVAULX

When the Cistercian monks chose a name for their new community they simply made a direct translation of 'Rye Vale' into French, coming up with 'Rievaulx' (pronounced 'Ree-vo').

The great choir of Rievaulx Abbey, built early in the 13th century, is still remarkably complete

RIEVAULX ABBEY   Map ref SE5785

A short drive (or pleasant stroll) from Helmsley is one of Yorkshire's finest treasures. Today the setting of Rievaulx Abbey (English Heritage) is sheltered and inviting, but when Walter l' Espec dispatched a group of French monks to find a suitable site on which to build a new community it was reported to be fit only for 'wild beasts and robbers'. At that time there were no roads in the area; instead of neat copses and lush meadows there were only impenetrable thickets. To the devoutly ascetic Cistercian monks this part of the Rye Valley represented the sort of challenge on which they thrived.

It was in the year 1131 that the monks began to build the mother church of the Cistercian Order in England.

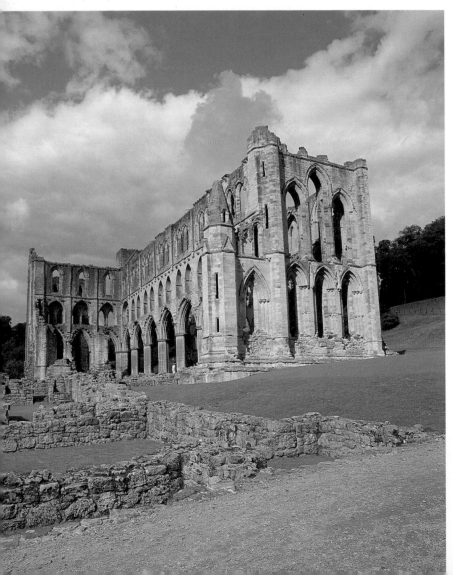

Many people today consider Rievaulx to be the pre-eminent Cistercian abbey in the country. The nave is Norman, while the rest of the abbey was built in the Early English style. Enough remains of all the buildings to give visitors a very clear impression of what monastic life was like all those centuries ago.

The monks may have started with an ascetic attitude to life; indeed the Cistercian Order was established in part due to what they considered to be the corruption of the Benedictines. But the 140 monks of Rievaulx (and as many as 600 lay brothers) succeeded in creating a community of great wealth and influence.

They farmed sheep; they grew vegetables; they ground corn. They smelted iron, a process which required the cutting down of perhaps 40 trees to make a hundredweight of metal. They even built a canal system (you follow it a short way during the Walk on page 70) to enable the iron to be transported by water. Stone for the buildings was brought to the site from local quarries by the same method. By 1538, when Henry VIII destroyed their way of life for ever, the monks had become very wealthy indeed.

Cut into the hillside above the abbey is Rievaulx Terrace (National Trust), a grassy promenade that is more than a match for the landscaped terrace at nearby Duncombe Park. The terrace at Rievaulx was designed in 1758. It offers strollers tantalising glimpses of the abbey between the groups of trees, with views of the Rye Valley and Hambleton Hills. There are temples, one in the Ionic style, the other Tuscan, to mark both ends of the terrace.

The abbey attracted other settlers to the valley, and its stones may be discovered in many local houses

THE VILLAGE

The delightful little village of Rievaulx, with its thatched cottages of honey-coloured stone, grew up only after the Reformation. It is rather ironic that many of the houses were built from stone salvaged from the ruins of the abbey.

The little houses of Stokesley present a charming mixture of styles

JOHN WRIGHTON
The seventh son of a seventh son is supposed to possess extraordinary powers. With this auspicious background, John Wrighton of Stokesley claimed curative powers that were little short of miraculous. During the first two decades of the 19th century he made a considerable reputation for curing ailments in both man and beast that had foxed more orthodox medics.
He told fortunes, advised the lovelorn, had stolen goods returned and saved people from the 'evil eye'. A magician's cloak, pointed hat and crystal ball completed Wrighton's outfit; small wonder that he was held in awe by country people.

STOKESLEY Map ref NZ5208
Now bypassed by the A172, Stokesley maintains the unhurried character of a market town. The broad verges of West Green create a little space between the Georgian façades of the houses and the main street that winds through the town. Stokesley still has regular markets, held every Friday on the cobbled edges of the main street. There are also busy livestock auctions and, each September, the market town is the site of one of the largest agricultural shows in the area.

The open spaces include College Square and the market square. Behind them is Levenside, where the River Leven, little more than a stream at this point, follows its tranquil course between grassy banks and underneath a succession of little bridges. The oldest of these is the handsome arch of an old packhorse bridge; near by is a ford.

With the re-drawing of the county boundaries in 1974, Stokesley had slipped into the county of Cleveland, though recently it has been brought back into North Yorkshire. The National Park boundary makes a detour to exclude the town and neighbouring Great Ayton. While many of Stokesley's inhabitants commute to industrial Teesdale immediately to the north, Stokesley has, nevertheless, kept its own identity.

The Cleveland Hills form a constant backdrop to the south as you drive northeast along the A172 between Osmotherley and Stokesley. Once frequented by drovers, packhorse men, pedlars and monks visiting their outlying granges, the paths of the Cleveland Hills are now used by weekend walkers.

SUTTON BANK   Map ref SE5183

The view from the top of Sutton Bank is one of the finest in Yorkshire. Below you, spread out like a vast picnic blanket, is the flat plain known as the Vale of York. It would be hard to imagine a sharper division between the rich, arable farmland to the south and the heather moors of the Hambleton Hills immediately to the north. On a clear day, armed with a pair of binoculars, you can see York Minster and the Three Peaks of the Yorkshire Dales. Gormire Lake, directly below and almost hidden by trees, was once imagined to be bottomless.

The A170 marks its midway point between the market towns of Thirsk and Helmsley by making a long 1-in-4 climb to the top of Sutton Bank. You can watch cars and lorries labouring up what is one of the steepest stretches of road in the country. For those who want to stretch their legs and enjoy the view, or for those whose engines overheat, there is a car park (and information centre) conveniently sited at the top.

From here there is a splendid, and undemanding, walk along the edge of Sutton Bank. The Yorkshire Gliding Club operates from the top of the bank, and on summer weekends the sky will be filled with slim, silent planes exploiting the thermals rising up the scar. Powered planes tow the gliders over the edge – a moment that will moisten the palms of all but the most nonchalant of flyers. With the addition of hang-gliders, microlight aircraft and soaring birds, the skies beyond Sutton Bank can get very busy indeed.

The walk continues along the top of Roulston Scar, offering beautiful views all the way, to the White Horse of Kilburn – one of those landmarks which looks better from a distance than up close. Thomas Taylor, a Kilburn

DROVERS' INNS

The Hambleton Inn, on the A170 about half a mile (800m) from the top of Sutton Bank, was once used by drovers bringing their cattle down from Scotland along the Hambleton Drove Road. There were three other drovers' inns on the moors, but they did not survive once the drovers stopped coming. Limekiln House is in ruins, Dialstone, near Sutton Bank (see side panel on next page) is now a farm. The Chequers pub, near Osmotherley, still bears its old chequerboard sign and the inscription:

'Be not in haste; Step in and taste;

Good ale for nothing – tomorrow.'

Enjoy the wonderful views across the Vale of York from Sutton Bank

DIALSTONE

Dialstone, a former drovers' inn and now a farm, was traditionally the site of the Hambleton Race Ground, where jockeys would compete for cups donated by patrons such as Queen Anne and George I. In the 18th century the Hambleton races eclipsed even those at York. The name Dialstone is thought to refer to the dial, or weighing machine, used before each horse-race for weighing the jockeys.

The highest ground for miles, Sutton Bank is a mecca for hang-gliders

man who made good in London, was so taken by the famous White Horse, cut into the chalk downs near Uffington, that he decided to create his own. He persuaded John Hodgson, a teacher from Kilburn School, to involve his pupils in the cutting of the figure. The main problem was that his chosen hillside, while suitably steep, was not chalk-based. Hodgson commandeered his pupils to help create the outline of a gigantic horse, and used gallons of whitewash to make the design stand out.

The White Horse of Kilburn is almost 325 feet (99m) from head to tail, and 227 feet (69m) in height. Finished in 1857 it is now the only major landscape figure in the north of England. Whitewash fades in time, of course, and ingenious efforts have been made down the years to find a suitable whitening agent; these days chalk chippings are used. A White Horse Fund has been set up for the purpose of maintaining the horse, which is a very distinctive and much-loved landmark for miles around.

There is another car park, directly beneath the White Horse, for those who don't want to walk too far. However you get to the horse, be careful not to damage the figure by walking on it.

The Western Moors

Leisure Information
Places of Interest
Shopping
Sports, Activities and
the Outdoors
Annual Events and Customs

Checklist

Leisure Information

TOURIST INFORMATION CENTRES

Helmsley
Market Place. Tel: 01439 770173.
Sutton Bank
Tel: 01845 597426.

OTHER INFORMATION

English Heritage (Yorkshire Region)
37 Tanner Row, York. Tel: 01904 601901.
www.english-heritage.org.uk
Environment Agency
Rivers House, 21 Park Square South, Leeds. Tel: 0113 2440191.
Forest Enterprise
Outgang Road, Pickering. Tel: 01751 472771.
National Trust
Goddards, 27 Tadcaster Road, York. Tel: 01904 702021.
North York Moors National Park
The Old Vicarage, Bondgate, Helmsley. Tel: 01439 770657.
Moorsbus summer coach and minibus
Tel 01439 770657.
Yorkshire Tourist Board
312 Tadcaster Road, York. Tel: 01904 707961.
Yorkshire Wildlife Trust
10 Toft Green, York. Tel: 01904 659570.

ORDNANCE SURVEY MAPS
Landranger 1:50,000. Sheets 93,100.

Places of Interest

There will be an admission charge at the following places of interest unless otherwise stated.
Byland Abbey
Coxwold. Tel: 01347 868614
Open Apr–Oct, daily; Nov–Mar most days.
Duncombe Park
Helmsley. Tel: 01439 770213.
Open May–Oct, Tue–Thu.
Gilling Castle
Gilling East. Tel: 01439 788238.
Open: Great Chamber and gardens daily in term time.
Helmsley Castle
Tel: 01439 770442. Open Apr–Oct, daily; Nov–Mar most days.
Helmsley Walled Garden
Tel: 01439 771427. Open Apr–Oct daily; wknds in winter.
Mount Grace Priory
Osmotherley. Tel: 01609 883494. Open Apr–Sep, daily; Oct–Mar, most days.
Newburgh Priory.
Tel: 01347 868435. Open Apr–Jun, Wed & Sun afternoons.
Rievaulx Abbey
Rievaulx. Tel: 01439 798228.
Open all year, daily.
Rievaulx Terrace
Rievaulx. Tel: 01439 798340.
Open Apr–Oct daily.

Shopping

Helmsley and Stokesley
Open-air market, Fri
Kirkbymoorside
Open-air market, Wed.

Sports, Activities and the Outdoors

LONG-DISTANCE FOOTPATHS

The Cleveland Way
A 110-mile (176-km) walk from Helmsley to Filey Brigg.
The Lyke Wake Walk
A 42-mile (67-km) walk from Beacon Hill to Ravenscar.

HORSE-RIDING

Hawnby
Bilsdale Riding Centre, Shaken Bridge Farm. Tel: 01439 798252.

Annual Events and Customs

Bilsdale
Bilsdale Show, Chop Gate, Aug.
Coxwold
Coxwold Fair, mid-June.
Helmsley
Ryedale Festival, July/August.
Kilburn
Kilburn Feast, early to mid-July.
Osmotherley
Summer Games, early July.
Osmotherley Show, August.
Stokesley
Stokesley Show, late September.

The Central Moors

The central moors include high moorland, beautiful valleys and some delectable villages. Rosedale Abbey hasn't got its abbey any more; the stones went to build the village when Rosedale boomed with the ironstone mines; now the valley is peaceful once again. Cropton Forest forms part of the North Riding Forest Park, and the Newtondale Drive offers panoramic views across the wooded Newtondale Gorge, through which steam trains run on the North Yorkshire Moors Railway. To the north of the forest is Wade's Causeway, a well-preserved section of road thought to be of Roman origin. The daffodils of Farndale are justifiably famous, but this is a lovely valley to visit at any time of year.

BACK TO NATURE

The recreational possibilities of Cropton Forest are now being realised. On any summer weekend you will see mountain bikers tackling the forest trails, walkers following well-waymarked footpaths and families enjoying themselves at the many picnic sites and adventure playgrounds. Those who prefer their nature 'red in tooth and claw' will head, instead, for the solitude of the breezy moor-tops. A new initiative is the Newtondale Horse Trail, offering 35 miles (56km) of bracing, traffic-free riding. Local riding stables hire out horses on an hourly or daily basis.

CROPTON FOREST

The moors are continually evolving, and one of the most dramatic changes this century has been the creation of large-scale conifer plantations. The Forestry Commission began the process in the 1920s; now the North Riding Forest Park comprises one of the most extensive man-made forests in the country.

Conifer planting on this scale has not met with universal approval; many feel that well-loved views have been smothered beneath the starkly geometric shapes of these plantations. Nevertheless, the afforestation of what had mostly been moorland and poor-quality farmland brought much-needed employment to many rural areas.

The woods are now reaching maturity, and upwards of 120,000 tonnes of timber are felled every year, meeting an ever-increasing need for softwoods. In recent years greater care has been taken to ensure that the plantations harmonise with their surroundings. Areas of broadleaved and mixed woodland provide a more varied habitat for wildlife, and are easier on the eye than conifer plantations.

Cropton Forest occupies a large area of the North Riding Forest Park between Rosedale in the west and Newtondale to the east. The easiest way to see the forest – and the wonderful views it affords down into the steep Newtondale gorge – is to take the Forest Drive. One point of access is Levisham Station, a halt on the North

Malo Cross, in Cropton Forest, marks an old crossing of the ways

Yorkshire Moors Railway, reached from the main A169 Pickering to Whitby road, via the delightful villages of Lockton and Levisham. Beyond Levisham the unfenced road winds steeply down to the station. The Forest Drive (toll payable) begins beyond the level crossing and ends near Mauley Cross.

Moorland crosses are generally reliable indicators that an old thoroughfare, or crossroads, is near at hand. Mauley Cross stands on the route of one of the oldest known roads across the moors to have survived.

Roman roads are not hard to find, on the map at least; Wade's Causeway on Wheeldale Moor, immediately to the north of Cropton Forest, may be that rare thing – a Roman road which is still visible on the ground.

There are Roman remains at Cawthorn Camp, which is signposted from the minor road between the villages of Cropton and Newton-on-Rawcliffe. From the purpose-built car park the waymarked path, no more than a mile (1.6km) long, guides you around them. The well-preserved earthworks reveal a camp, two forts and an annexe wedged side by side on a plateau which enjoys panoramic views to the north, across Cropton Forest to the moors beyond. By the year AD 122, when the Emperor Hadrian was constructing his famous wall to the north, the Cawthorn camps had been abandoned.

THE NEWTONDALE FOREST DRIVE

The single-track road from Levisham accompanies the North Yorkshire Moors Railway before climbing steeply; views soon open up on the right of Newton Dale, with the Hole of Horcum, a dramatic landform, beyond the immediate horizon. If time is not pressing, park at the top and enjoy the view; with luck you may see one of the steam-hauled trains on the line. The Newtondale Halt, way below you, has no road access, making it the most isolated station on this most scenic of restored lines. The drive continues through Cropton Forest, meeting a public road once again near Mauley Cross.

The dales are rich in folklore; one story tells of Kitty Garthwaite, 'Sarkless Kitty', from the village of Lowna Bridge, who, two centuries ago, was 'walking out' with Willie Dixon of Hutton-le-Hole. A rumour came to Kitty that Willie was seeing another lass. A lovers' tiff by the River Dove was followed, tragically, by Kitty being found drowned in a pool, wearing only her 'sark', or petticoat. After their argument, Willie had ridden to York to get a marriage licence. On his return his horse stumbled and Willie drowned in the same pool where Kitty had earlier been found. The ghost of Kitty, naked but carrying her sark over her arm, began to haunt the riverside spot where the lovers had kept their trysts.

Daffodils carpet the ground in a spectacular springtime show in Farndale

FARNDALE

Farndale is a delightful valley at any time of the year, but every Easter it blooms with a profusion of wild daffodils. The daffodil walk accompanies the River Dove between Low Mill and Church Houses. This is an undeniably pleasant stroll, and suitable for wheelchairs, but try to pick a weekday, if possible, to make your visit; or venture a little further afield, for wild daffodils can be found throughout the valley. The traffic has become so heavy in recent years that a field in the village of Low Mill becomes a car park while the daffodils are in bloom. A recent initiative is a park-and-ride bus service operating from Kirkbymoorside and Hutton-le-Hole.

But why Farndale? And why in such profusion? Farndale's blooms are wild, short-stemmed daffodils; stories variously attribute their planting to the monks of Rievaulx, and to Father Postgate, a Catholic priest who was persecuted for his faith. We merely know that wild daffodils have flourished in these dales for centuries.

The greatest threat to them has been the ever-increasing numbers of visitors, who were unable to admire the springtime displays without gathering armfuls of flowers. Once market traders found this free source of daffodils the flowers were in danger, and in 1953 about 2,000 acres of Farndale were designated as a nature reserve; the daffodils are safe for us all to enjoy. Resist the temptation to pick any.

At other times of the year Farndale reverts to being a peaceful farming community. Both sides of the valley are accessible; from either Kirkbymoorside and Hutton-le-Hole to the south, or, most dramatically, from the north down a steep road which descends from Blakey Ridge just to the south of the Lion Inn.

HOVINGHAM Map ref SE6675

One of North Yorkshire's prettiest villages, Hovingham lies on the route of an old Roman road from Malton to Boroughbridge. When the foundations of Hovingham Hall were being laid, in 1745, Roman remains were unearthed, including part of a bath house. The Hall's first owner, Sir Thomas Worseley, was a direct descendant of Oliver Cromwell. His passion for horses led him to build the Hall's stable block facing on to the village green. In an unusual arrangement, visitors have to pass through the stable block to reach the Hall's main entrance. The Hall is open to parties only.

The architectural unity of the surrounding houses, the neat layout with broad grass verges and an air of gentility all mark Hovingham out as an estate village. One of the Hall's lawns is the village's cricket pitch; surely one of the loveliest grounds on which to watch or play the summer game. The houses at the northern end of the village are clustered either side of a little beck, where ducks swim and await visitors who may have stale bread to feed to them.

HUTTON-LE-HOLE Map ref SE7090

It's to Hutton-le-Hole's benefit that it lies just off the main A170 between Thirsk and Scarborough, for it has managed to maintain its distinctive personality instead of merely selling its soul to the tourist trade. One of Yorkshire's 'picture postcard' villages, its houses are set back from Hutton Beck, a little watercourse spanned by a succession of pretty little bridges. The village green is the size of a meadow, but the grass is cropped short by grazing sheep which wander proprietorially wherever they choose – as likely as not in the middle of the road.

The houses of discreet grey stone, with the red-tiled roofs so typical of the moors, lend a timeless air to the village. The tiny church has some fine oak furniture made by Robert Thompson of Kilburn; a close examination will reveal the carved mice that were his distinctive trademark.

Once you have seen the village, don't neglect to explore the Ryedale Folk Museum. This fascinating open-

RYEDALE'S WITCH POST

The cruck-framed house at the Ryedale Folk Museum contains one of the few examples of a witch post to have survived – most of which are in the north of England. This post, of mountain ash, is elaborately carved with a cross and other, more ambiguous, symbols. It stands by the fireplace, so it would be passed by everyone who came into the living area, and also had the more practical purpose of supporting the beam across the inglenook. Its purpose was, of course, to ward off evil spirits and protect those who sat here enjoying the fire's warmth.

Hutton-le-Hole, rimed in frost and wreathed in the mist of early morning

CRUCK-FRAMED HOUSES
The crucks and their cross-beams made a shape like the letter 'A'; these heavy timbers supported the entire weight of the building's roof, allowing the walls to be infilled. Since the walls were not load-bearing, it was an easy matter to alter the position of doors, or create extra windows.

air collection is based on the displays of bygones built up by two local collectors. From its beginnings in a single old farm building, the museum has expanded far beyond its walls, to include many other vernacular buildings – brought stone by stone to the museum and painstakingly re-erected.

For nearly 500 years a small, thatched, cruck-framed cottage stood in the village of Danby. In 1967 this typical farmer's house was moved to the museum's 2½-acre (1-ha) site. The tall, 16th-century manor house, also thatched and cruck-framed, is a huge hall open to the roof beams. This was once the meeting place of the Manor Court, where disputes were settled and common rights safeguarded. Other museum buildings house a photographer's studio, a primitive 16th-century glass furnace and a row of shops recreated as they would have looked more than a century ago.

Throughout these buildings, exhibits in their own right, are informal displays showing what life was like in such moorland villages during bygone days.

KIRKBYMOORSIDE Map ref SE6986
The market town of Kirkbymoorside lies just outside the National Park, on the A170 between Helmsley and Pickering. Don't judge the place by first appearances; you should leave the main road to investigate the old heart of the town. The broad main street is lined with inns, a reminder that Kirkbymoorside was an important halt in the days of stage coaches. The oldest inn is the Black Swan, whose elaborately carved entrance porch bears the date 1632. The market cross, mounted on a stepped base,

can be found in a side street near by. Market day is Wednesday, as it has been since medieval times.

Kirkbymoorside has a road called Castlegate. Once it had a castle too, on a hill behind the parish church, but stones salvaged from its ruins were used to build the 17th-century tollbooth. Another fortified building was once a hunting lodge built by the Neville family. The church, though old, was largely rebuilt last century.

Lovers of beautiful old churches should rejoin the A170 westwards in the direction of Helmsley for just a few hundred yards, before following the sign for St Gregory's Minster. If the word 'minster' conjures up some grand edifice, you will be surprised to find a tiny, dignified church of grey stone, almost hidden away in beautiful, secluded Kirkdale.

This ancient building was dedicated to St Gregory – the pope who sent St Augustine to preach Christianity to the pagan English in AD 597. There has long been a church here, certainly before Anglo-Saxon times, as it needed rebuilding in c1060, perhaps as a result of Viking destruction. Recent excavations have revealed a prehistoric standing stone by the west tower, evidence of Christians observing a pagan rite. Many visitors ask: why a minster? And why here, in such an isolated spot? The term 'minster' is derived from the Latin *monasterium* which denoted a community of priests or monks who used the church as a base from which to serve the surrounding countryside before the parish system evolved. This status has remained with churches; some like this one are small, some like York Minster are large and important.

We can be more certain about the dates of the rebuilding because ancient – yet tantalisingly brief – details are carved on a sundial mounted over the south door. The sun doesn't reach it any more; to protect the sundial, the best Anglo-Saxon example known, a porch was added in the 19th century.

ST GREGORY'S SUNDIAL

The inscription on the sundial at St Gregory's Minster is in Old English. Translated it reads 'Orm, the son of Gamal, bought St Gregory's Church when it was utterly broken down and fallen, and he rebuilt it from ground level, to Christ and St Gregory, in the days of King Edward and Earl Tostig. Howarth made me and Brand the priest. This is sun's marker at all times'.

The Edward of the inscription is King Edward the Confessor, who ruled between 1042 and 1066; Tostig became Earl of Northumberland in 1055; Howarth made the sundial; Brand was the parish priest. This brief inscription is the longest example of Anglo-Saxon carving to have survived.

The extensive porch on St Gregory's Minster protects an ancient inscribed sundial

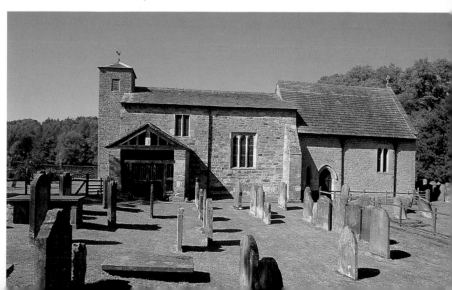

Lastingham and Hutton-le-Hole

A short walk beneath Spaunton Moor, linking two of the loveliest villages within the National Park. Leave time to look around the fascinating Ryedale Folk Museum at Hutton-le-Hole.

Time: 2 hours. Distance: 4 miles (6.4km).
Location: 6 miles (9.7km) northwest of Pickering.
Start: Park in Lastingham village. (OS grid ref: SE729904.)
OS Map: Outdoor Leisure 26 (North York Moors – Western area) 1:25,000.
See Key to Walks on page 123.

ROUTE DIRECTIONS

From **Lastingham** walk in the direction of Cropton and Pickering. As the road bears

The Ryedale Folk Museum has an open-air section with farming displays and a number of restored buildings, including a medieval long-house

left, go right (signed as a cul-de-sac), to cross a little bridge. Follow Ings Beck for a few yards past cottages and when the metalled road peters out, bear right, uphill, on to a broad path into woodland.

At the top of the wood pass through a wooden gate, to come out shortly at a road

junction. Take the road signposted 'Spaunton', soon reaching its scattering of houses. Pass a cottage with a 1695 datestone, then follow the road round to the right. Almost immediately, follow a footpath sign to the left towards Grange Farm. Keep to the right of a big barn and walk through the farmyard, then follow the track right and then left. As you approach more big barns veer left and then right by a stone wall. The track is easy walking, slightly uphill between a fence and a wall, with fine views opening up on your left.

At two isolated trees, the track veers left and then right, past a ruined farm building, the track now narrowing into a path hemmed in by unruly hedgerows. As the path veers left leave it by a gap in the hedge into a field as Hutton-le-Hole is seen ahead. After just a few yards, take a gate to your left, and follow a path as it twists steeply downhill. You are

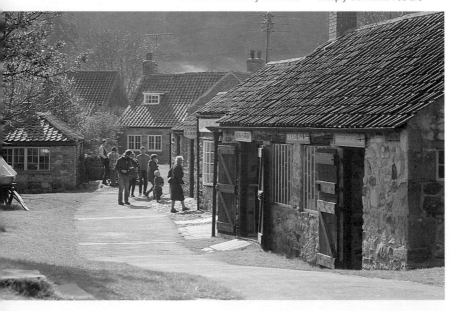

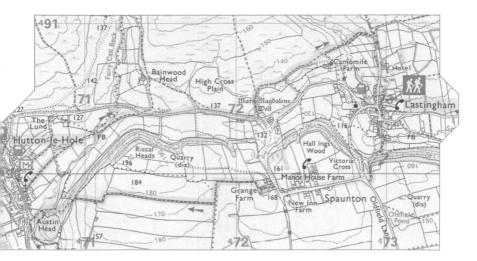

guided by yellow arrows past a beck into the village of **Hutton-le-Hole**.

For the return half of the walk, after exploring this delightful village, locate the village hall and follow a footpath sign on the opposite side of the road. A snicket (narrow path between walls and/or fences) takes you around the village bowling green, past the tiny church and out into open fields. Follow a fence along the left edge of a field, then cross three fields and stiles to a footbridge over Fairy Call Beck. Follow the path uphill, into a small wood. Go through a gate and follow the grassy track to a road.

Bear right, along the quiet road with wide verges. Just before the road sweeps downhill to the right, follow a footpath sign on your left, up a grassy track and through a gate. Bear right with open moorland to your left and fields to your right. Keep left of a prominent clump of trees and Camomile Farm to follow a wall steeply downhill, over the beck and equally steeply uphill to a junction of tracks. There is a bench here, so that

weary walkers can sit and drink in the view. Take the track to the right, downhill, through a gate and back to Lastingham and the start of the walk.

POINTS OF INTEREST

Lastingham
Lastingham (see page 86) is an attractive little village almost hidden in the folds of the surrounding hills. St Mary's Church has an impressive Norman crypt dedicated to St Cedd and one of the wellheads dotted around the village also bears his name. If you take this walk in the morning, you'll be able to explore neighbouring Hutton-le-Hole and still have time to get back to Lastingham for a leisurely lunch – perhaps at the Blacksmith's Arms opposite the church.

Hutton-le-Hole
Here is another candidate for the title of Yorkshire's prettiest village. The houses of mellow local stone are grouped unselfconsciously round the green that extends the length of the village, lending it a

distinctive character. In the centre of Hutton-le-Hole (see page 81) is the Ryedale Folk Museum: a fascinating collection of bygones housed in a variety of buildings. Leave an hour, at least, to explore the museum.

The Blacksmith's Arms, opposite Lastingham's church, offers refreshment for thirsty walkers

The extraordinary crypt in the church at Lastingham is supported by stout Norman pillars

PRAYERS AND PINTS

Lastingham's church and pub are just a few yards apart; at one time the links were even closer. During the 18th century Reverend Carter combined his duties as a minister with helping his wife to dispense pints at the pub, and playing a few tunes on his violin. With 13 children to feed, he found the church stipend of £20 insufficient on its own to keep body and soul together. He claimed 'My parishioners derive a triple advantage, being instructed, fed and amused at the same time'.

LASTINGHAM Map ref SE7290

The casual visitor to Lastingham will see a collection of good-looking houses, a few wellheads and a welcoming inn, but Lastingham has something more to offer – a unique place in the history of Christianity.

St Cedd left Lindisfarne in AD 655 and chose this site on which to build a monastery. It was an area which, according to the Venerable Bede, was 'the lurking place of robbers and wild beasts'. St Cedd was buried in his monastery, close to the altar. This early building was later sacked by invading Danes.

In 1078 Abbot Stephen of Whitby moved his own community to Lastingham. He built a crypt dedicated to St Cedd, in which the saint's remains were re-interred. Apart from cosmetic changes (and the stairs leading down into it from the nave of the church above) the crypt looks the way it did almost a thousand years ago.

Itself a church in miniature, the crypt has stout Norman pillars, a low vaulted roof and a stone slab for an altar. Here, too, are fragments of ancient crosses. It was to have been part of a large abbey, but Abbot Stephen's plans were thwarted and the community moved to the larger site of St Mary's Abbey, York.

The present church, planned merely as the abbey's chancel, was eventually consolidated to meet local needs; the congregation was derived from those who lived in many of the surrounding villages. Today, visitors to Lastingham's church come from further afield to see a building that has happily survived years of neglect and clumsy 'restorations'. A closer examination of two of the village's wellheads reveal that one is dedicated to St Cedd, the other to his brother, St Chad, who succeeded him as Abbot of Lastingham.

NUNNINGTON   Map ref SE6679

At Nunnington a delightful 17th-century three-arched bridge spans the River Rye. From one of its embrasures (the V-shaped spaces constructed to shield pedestrians from the traffic) you can gaze down into the water and try to spot basking trout, superbly camouflaged against the sandy river bed. Across the water is Nunnington Hall. This tranquil setting offers no clue to the hall's turbulent past; this isn't one of those stately homes which cruised serenely through the centuries, while leaving barely a ripple.

The hall's early history is sketchy; it is thought to have been built on the site of a nunnery – hence its name. It passed through many hands, including the Abbot of St Mary's, York. A later owner, Viscount Preston, served James II as Secretary of State for Scotland; charged later with treason, he only escaped the gallows by implicating his fellow conspirators.

While the hall's west wing can be dated to 1580, most of the building, a concoction of Tudor and Stuart styles, was built during the 17th century. The Hall, housing the entrancing Carlisle collection of miniature rooms and a display by the British Toymakers Guild, is now in the hands of the National Trust.

Nunnington's handsome houses in grey stone are hidden from sight to those who drive straight through the village; it's better to explore on foot. Nunnington's church, with its double dedication to St James and All Saints, dates largely from the 13th century. Here, in an alcove, is the effigy of a knight in chain mail. This recumbent figure commemorates Sir Walter de Teyes, Lord of the Manor of Nunnington and Stonegrave until his death in 1325.

NUNNINGTON'S DRAGON-SLAYER

In 1065 Peter Loschy, a brave knight, rode off with his dog to kill a dragon in its lair. Wounds inflicted on the dragon healed up by magic so when Loschy hacked off a piece of the dragon, his dog would carry it off before it healed. Spitting poison to the end, the dragon was killed with a mighty blow that severed its head from its body. The mastiff carried off the dragon's head then jumped up and licked his master's face; unfortunately the dragon's poison was still on the dog's jowls. In seconds both were dead.

The lovely old manor house of Nunnington Hall is beautifully set in gardens near the river

Between 1850 and 1870 the population of Rosedale quadrupled, as the mines were driven deep into the valley sides. A system of underground passages were dug, consolidated by wooden supports. The miners excavated to either side of these tunnels, with pick and shovel, to win the ore-bearing rock. The news soon spread, with experienced miners converging on Rosedale from all over the country – and particularly from Cornwall and Wales. At the height of production, more than 5,000 men found work here.

THE NUNNERY
In the garden at Rosedale Abbey, immediately beyond the church's west door, are the remains of a tower with a spiral staircase inside. The nuns would have climbed these steps to reach their dormitory. The nunnery was dissolved in 1535, though the buildings remained standing until the ironstone mining boom created a sudden need for building stone.

CYCLING IN ROSEDALE
The old Rosedale railway is ideal for cycling for much of its length, as it is relatively level and surfaced with ash ballast. The best section is from Rosedale Bank Top to Blakey Junction, near the Lion Inn (4 miles/6.8km) and then across the moors to Ingleby Bank Top another 7 miles (11.9km). You could even cycle down the incline – but remember what goes down must come up again.

ROSEDALE

Rosedale is a tranquil valley today, echoing with the bubbling cry of the curlew and the distant barking of farm dogs. City visitors will feel themselves to be a very long way from the noise and grime of Yorkshire's industrial heartlands. But appearances can be deceptive. A hundred years ago the scene was very different: Rosedale was a veritable moorland 'Klondyke'.

Ironstone had been mined here, sporadically, since the Iron Age. During the 13th century mining certainly added to the wealth of the monks of Byland Abbey; but it was only in the middle of the 19th century that the extent of Rosedale's subterranean wealth was realised, with the discovery of massive quantities of top-grade iron ore. The Industrial Revolution brought a huge demand for iron; the blast furnaces on the Rivers Tees and Tyne needed a constant supply for building ships, railways and general engineering. Other mines were driven – at Glaisdale, Beck Hole and on the coast, for example – but the mines at Rosedale proved to be the most productive.

The transport of ore was difficult from isolated Rosedale. In 1861 the North Eastern Railway Company built a line from Battersby Junction on the Stockton–Whitby line, over the bleak moorland to Rosedale West. In 1865 a branch was built around the head of Rosedale to the east mines, joining the original line at Blakey Junction, just below the Lion Inn on Blakey Ridge. To reach Teesside the wagons, laden with ore, were winched down the steep descent of the Ingleby Incline. The engines that plied the high-level line between the Rosedale mines and the incline never came down from their moorland heights, except when they had to be repaired.

The Rosedale railway was closed in 1929, by which time the valley's mining boom was over. Though the demand for iron was as buoyant as ever, ore could be mined more cheaply elsewhere. The route of this fascinating line can still be seen; the Walk on page 90 crosses its path. The valley is quietly 'going back to nature', but the massive calcining kilns (where ironstone was roasted to reduce its weight) are being consolidated, so that Rosedale's mining past will not be forgotten.

You will search in vain for the abbey that gave the village of Rosedale Abbey its name. The ladies who serve in the teashops answer the question with a weary resignation that suggests this is not the first time they've been asked. The truth is that you can see the remains of the abbey (it was actually a priory) wherever you look: the population explosion of the mid-19th century meant that the priory was plundered for its building stone to build homes for the ironstone miners. Whether this is seen as the desecration of a religious site, or the sensible recycling of a valuable resource, depends on your own reading of history. The priory was founded in 1158 as a

Cistercian nunnery by William of Rosedale. Never a large establishment, there were probably only nine nuns and a prioress living here.

St Lawrence's Church stands on the site of the priory's chapel. To find a couple of relics from the earlier building, walk up to the altar rail. One of the stones set into the floor bears a carved cross and, faintly, the name Maria, in memory of one of the nuns. Beyond the altar rail is an ancient stone seat from the nunnery; it is carved from a single block of stone.

Rosedale, one of the largest and prettiest valleys of the moors, attracts visitors throughout the year

The Head of Rosedale

A bracing circuit around both sides of the beautiful valley of Rosedale. Moorland alternates with fields and drystone walls and the valley floor is punctuated by solitary farmsteads.

Time: 3½ hours. Distance: 6 miles (9.7km).
Location: 11 miles (17.7km) northwest of Pickering.
Start: Park on Blakey Ridge, by the turn-off to Farndale, just over half a mile (1km) south of the Lion Inn.
(OS grid ref: SE684989.)
OS Map: Outdoor Leisure 26 (North York Moors – Western area) 1:25,000.
See Key to Walks on page 123.

ROUTE DIRECTIONS

From the parking place follow a footpath sign down into Rosedale to the trackbed of the old **Rosedale Railway**. Cross it, continue ahead, downhill, towards a pair of farms in the valley. Soon you meet a farm track; follow it to the right, downhill, through a gate to Moorlands Farm. Keep left of an outbuilding with a

The view down the valley of Rosedale

pigeon loft in its eaves. Keep left of a smaller outbuilding, go through a gate and continue to Hollin Bush Farm. Follow the track around farm buildings, then go right, over the right-hand wall stile next to a gate.

Follow the wall, downhill, towards another farm ahead. At the bottom of the field go steeply down to a footbridge over a beck, then continue uphill crossing a field to join a metalled track at Dale Head

Farm. Turn left on to the track. On your right is a signpost 'Bridleway to Gt Fryup Dale'. Go through the gate, follow the path around a barn. Your route soon becomes a more substantial track leading uphill, between fences, through a small wooded valley.

On reaching a broader track, follow it to the right, still uphill, to cross again the trackbed of the old railway. Follow the path uphill keeping the stream on your right. At the head of the valley where the path forks, follow the right-hand path to an old guide stone ('Whitby' on one side and 'Rosedale' the other). Keep straight ahead, uphill, following the stakes, to an unfenced moorland road. Turn right on this road. With wide verges and little traffic this is easy, level walking.

Look for a bridleway sign on the right. From here cross open moor, back down into Rosedale aiming for a stubby stone chimney, slightly to the left on the immediate horizon. When you reach the chimney you will find other relics of the **ironstone industry**: particularly an impressive row of kilns and the remains of the rail system that transported wagon-loads of ironstone.

Walk to the rear of the kilns, passing a big spoil-heap, to join the main railway trackbed. Walk left along it as it becomes a stony track that keeps left of the old Rosedale goods station buildings. Go through a gate, pass a farmhouse and reach a road. Turn right to pass Ebeneezer Primitive Methodist Chapel (dated 1872). At the next house (B&B), turn left and pass holiday cottages. Go through a farmyard to the gate at the far side, and follow the field edge downhill,

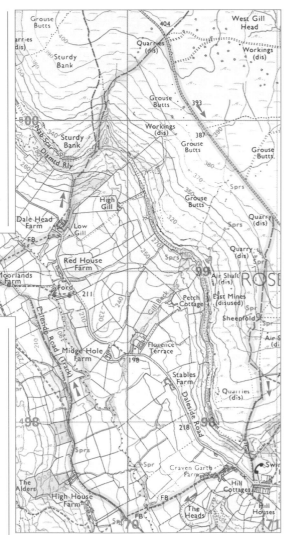

towards a farm on the opposite side of the valley.

Cross a stile, go through a gate and descend to a footbridge over a beck. Walk uphill to a gate, then turn right along a farm track to pass below High House Farm and then a ruined farmstead. Continue along the track (marked Daleside Road on the map), skirting a wood. Where the track forks take the lowest right-hand fork. Pass through a succession of gates and eventually emerge on to a very minor road. Turn left towards Moorlands Farm once again. Pass between the farm buildings to a gate; retrace your steps up the steep track to the top of Blakey Ridge and your car.

POINTS OF INTEREST

The Rosedale Railway
During the second half of the 19th century Rosedale rang with the noise of iron-ore mining. The railway line was built in 1861, specifically to transport mined ore to the blast-furnaces of Teesside. Trains ran round the Rosedale skyline, before leaving at a junction (where you parked your car) and heading north. The wagons were lowered down an incline to join the main line to Middlesbrough while the engines themselves stayed on the moor-top, except when needing repair. Today the trackbed of the railway is a concessionary path.

Ironstone Workings
Set into the side of the steep valley are the 16 arches of the πkilns still stand, seeming to gaze across the valley. These important relics (and another set of kilns in the vicinity) are in the process of being consolidated, to prevent further collapse.

The Roman road on Wheeldale is commonly known as Wade's Causeway. This is yet another reference to a giant who, according to legend, created many of the landforms on the moors. Wade was a genuine figure in northern history; his skirmishes, during the 9th century, made him a folk hero. The giant Wade of legend and his wife Bell built a road across the moorland. Bell carried rocks in her apron; whenever she spilt a load, a rocky hill would be instantly created. The legendary road followed the course of the Roman road, which by the 9th century was more than seven hundred years old.

High on Wheeldale Moor lies a stretch of ancient road known as Wade's Causeway

WHEELDALE

The Romans made few incursions into what we now know as the North York Moors. The inescapable conclusion is that the wastes of 'Blackamore' held few attractions for the colonists. However, they may have built a road across the moors to link a settlement at Malton with the signal stations on the coast near Goldsborough and Whitby.

A section of road on Wheeldale Moor, just over a mile (1.6km) in length and known as Wade's Causeway, is reckoned to be the best-preserved Roman road in the country, though doubts have been expressed in recent years about its Roman origins. The road gradually fell into disuse, eventually disappearing beneath the encroaching heather and bracken. It was rediscovered as recently as 1914. It can be reached by driving north from Pickering on an unclassified road. Once past the village of Stape, follow the Wheeldale Road with Cropton Forest on the right and the expanse of Wheeldale Moor to the left. Park near the watersplash at Wheeldale Bridge, and the old Roman road is immediately ahead. Wade's Causeway is also signposted from the village of Goathland, west of the A169.

We all learned about the Romans' road-making skills at school, yet this road looks a very rocky thoroughfare. That's simply because what we can see today was merely the road's original foundation, made up of large stones set into gravel. The road surface would have been much smoother, overlaid with finer aggregate. The road is cambered so that water would drain off to the edges and be carried away in culverts. You can follow the route and decide for yourself whether or not you are walking in the footsteps of those Roman legions.

MOORLAND CROSSES

It is appropriate that Ralph Cross should have been chosen as the emblem of the National Park, for standing stones and wayside crosses are one of the most intriguing features of the moors. No other area of the country can boast so many examples.

Within the National Park there are more than a thousand stones raised by man, standing witness to many centuries of settlement on the moors. The moorland stones are known as 'crosses', even though only a small proportion of them are actually carved into the shape of a cross. Some are simple monoliths fitted with side-pieces to make a cruciform shape. One particular design, repeated in many moorland crosses, is known as the wheelhead. It consisted of a widening of the top of a stone, which is pierced with four holes to create the shape of a cross. Others stones simply have the design of a cross carved into their surface.

The moorland crosses weren't erected at random; they were put up for a variety of reasons, which only adds to their interest. A number of them were preaching crosses, marking the spot where itinerant monks would attempt to bring the gospel to the pagan Anglo-Saxon communities. If the monks were successful and their words fell on willing ears, a church might eventually be built on, or near, the site of the preaching cross.

In the Middle Ages other crosses were put up as waymarkers, to guide travellers across the largely featureless expanses of 'Blackamore'. The moorland roads were established by usage only; they weren't 'built' like the Roman roads; at best, the routes might be

Ana Cross, a striking landmark on Spaunton Moor, also provides a handy seat for wayfarers

EARLY SIGNPOSTS

Signposts of stone were erected at all crossroads on the moors in 1711 by order of the Justices at Northallerton, to prevent travellers getting lost on the moors. They give the direction of each road to the nearest main town, and sometimes distances. The spelling is distinctly idiosyncratic, and some have primitive hands carved on them. There is a good example about 2 miles (3.2km) north out of Hutton-le-Hole on the road to Ralph Cross at SE693926.

LILLA CROSS

The oldest cross on the moors is reckoned to be Lilla Cross, situated off the Whitby–Pickering road at Ellerbeck Bridge. Possibly of 10th-century provenance, it is said to mark the final resting place of Lilla, a minister to King Edwin, whose kingdom encompassed the Yorkshire Wolds. Lilla saved the life of his king by falling on to the sword of a would-be assassin, but died in the process. The story goes that King Edwin commemorated this selfless act with the cross you can still see today.

THE CROSSES WALK

The Crosses Walk is a challenge walk of about 53 miles (84.8km), created to be undertaken in a single day. Starting and finishing at the village of Goathland, it uses thirteen prominent crosses for their original purpose, as waymarkers.

delineated by a line of causeway stones. The moorland crosses would help to mark the route, and offer weary travellers further targets in the distance to aim for. Other crosses were erected to mark the boundaries of the monastic sheep-grazing land.

During these times the building of bridges and wayside crosses was seen as an act of piety. Many rich men would attempt to improve their chances of getting into heaven by providing money for such good works. So, here too, a stone shaped as a cross would reflect both the donor's good intentions and the travellers' gratitude to find another waymark. It's hard for us, cosseted in our cars, to imagine how reassuring it would have been to see a moorland cross appear through the mist. The spiritual aspect of these moorland crosses was further emphasised by the custom of leaving coins on them – many had an indentation on the top – for needy travellers.

Many crosses now exist only as empty stone 'sockets' or names featured on old maps. Nevertheless, at least 30 moorland crosses still stand to their full height. Ralph Cross, at 9 feet (2.75m) high on the top of Blakey Ridge, is also known as Young Ralph. It has been a familiar landmark for centuries, since it marks a meeting of important tracks. Now it can be seen by motorists driving between Castleton and Hutton-le-Hole. In 1961 Ralph Cross was damaged by a man clambering up to check for coins. Vandals did more damage, but repairs have restored it to its former glory. Close by are two more crosses: 'Old Ralph' is a mere four feet (1.2m) high, while 'Fat Betty' comprises a rounded stone 'head' on a square stone 'body'.

The squat little cross known as 'Fat Betty' is whitewashed to enable it to be seen across the moor

The Central Moors

Leisure Information
Places of Interest
Shopping
Sports, Activities and the Outdoors
Annual Events and Customs

Checklist

Leisure Information

TOURIST INFORMATION CENTRES

Hutton-le-Hole
Ryedale Folk Museum.
Tel· 01751 417367.

OTHER INFORMATION

English Heritage (Yorkshire Region)
37 Tanner Row, York. Tel: 01904 601901.
www.english-heritage.org.uk
Environment Agency
Rivers House, 21 Park Square South, Leeds. Tel: 0113 2440191.
Forest Enterprise
Outgang Road, Pickering.
Tel: 01751 472771.
National Trust
Goddards, 27 Tadcaster Road, York. Tel: 01904 702021.
www.nationaltrust.org.uk
North York Moors National Park Centre
The Old Vicarage, Bondgate, Helmsley. Tel: 01439 770657.
Moorsbus summer coach and minibus
Tel 01439 770657.
www.moorsbus.net
Yorkshire Tourist Board
312 Tadcaster Road, York.

Tel: 01904 707961.
www.ytb.org.uk
Yorkshire Wildlife Trust
10 Toft Green, York. Tel: 01904 659570.

ORDNANCE SURVEY MAPS

Landranger 1:50,000. Sheets 93, 94, 100.

Places of Interest

There will be an admission charge at the following places of interest unless otherwise stated.
Cawthorne
Remains of Roman camp on road between Cropton and Newton-on-Rawcliffe. Open daily. Free.
Nunnington Hall
Nunnington. Tel: 01439 748283. Open Apr–Oct, most days.
Ryedale Folk Museum
Hutton-le-Hole. Tel: 01751 417367. Open Mar–Oct, daily.

Shopping

LOCAL SPECIALITIES

Glass
Gillies Jones Glass Design, The Old Forge, Rosedale Abbey.
Tel: 01751 417550.

Sports, Activities and the Outdoors

HORSE-RIDING

Newtondale Horse Trail
35 traffic-free miles (56km) in the North Riding Forest Park.
Sinnington
Friars Hill Riding Stables.
Tel. 01751 432758.

MOUNTAIN BIKE HIRE

Bike It!, Gales House Farm.
Tel: 01751 431258.
Cropton Forest. Tel: 01751 417510 (summer only).

WATERSPORTS

Sutherland Lodge Activity Centre, Cropton. Tel: 01751 417228. Canoeing.

Annual Events and Customs

Hutton-le-Hole World Merrills Championships, (board game) mid-September.
Farndale Farndale Show, late August.
Rosedale Rosedale Show, mid-August.
Ryedale Ryedale Show, Kirkbymoorside, late July.

The Eastern Moors and the Coast

This section covers the eastern moors, a triangle formed between Whitby, Scarborough and Pickering. The coastline offers spectacular cliffs, hidden coves, sandy beaches and rock formations that continue to fascinate geologists. Bird-watchers will find a wealth of sea birds nesting on the cliff ledges, and soaring far out to sea. To preserve the area's unique character, many miles have been declared as a Heritage Coast. Robin Hood's Bay is one of the loveliest fishing villages in the country, whilst Scarborough is Yorkshire's premier seaside resort. Another 'must' is a ride on the restored North Yorkshire Moors Railway, steam-hauled trains taking you deep into the moors.

EBBERSTON HALL

Midway between Brompton and Thornton-le-Dale is the village of Ebberston. On the opposite side of the road is Ebberston Hall, a stately home built in the Palladian style... but a stately home almost in miniature. The Hall was built in 1718 for William Thompson, MP for Scarborough, with the purpose (so the story goes) of winning a lady's affections. Today it remains a perfect example of classical symmetry, albeit with a mere eleven rooms.

BROMPTON   Map ref SE9482

Motorists on the A170 tend to drive straight through the village of Brompton in their haste to get to the coast. William Wordsworth took the time to get to know it better, for he courted Mary Hutchinson, a local girl who lived at Gallows Hill Farm. When they married, in 1802, it was in Brompton's own 14th-century church. The ceremony was recorded in her diary by his sister Dorothy; she even joined the happy couple on their honeymoon in Grasmere, Cumbria.

Gallows Hill, on the A170 between Brompton and Wykeham, is now the Wordsworth Gallery devoted to fine arts and gifts. Upstairs is an exhibition about the life and work of William Wordsworth, and his connections with Gallows Hill.

The village has a unique (though sadly little-known) place in the history of aeronautics. Everybody knows it was Wilbur and Orville Wright who made the first manned flight, in their flimsy craft, *Kittyhawk*. Yet a remarkable 50 years before that memorable occasion, an unsung squire of Brompton Hall quietly set about building a flying machine.

Brompton Hall (now an independent school and not open to the public) had been the home of the Cayley family since Stuart times, and Sir George Cayley (1771–1857) developed an unquenchable scientific curiosity. This was an age when enthusiastic amateurs, especially those blessed with private incomes, could indulge their whims in the arts and sciences. Sir George, however, was no mere dabbler; his inventions included caterpillar tracks and a new form of artificial limb, prompted by an accident to one of his estate workers. Seeing how the River Derwent regularly flooded the surrounding flat countryside, to the chagrin of local farmers, he designed and constructed a sea cut to divert flood waters straight into the North Sea near Scarborough (see Walk on page 100).

But flight remained Sir George's grand passion. Even before the 18th century was out he was designing gliders – continuing to refine the aerodynamics until he had a controllable craft that could carry a man. Remarkably, he had already experimented with propellers, abandoning them merely because the internal combustion engine was not even on the horizon. His experiments proved that a contoured wing could provide much greater lift than a wing with a flat profile.

Though an inscription in the church porch acknowledges Sir George as the 'Father of Aeronautics', his pioneering efforts are still largely overlooked. Facing the main road through the village is the six-sided building, boarded up, unfortunately, where Sir George worked on his flying machines.

A RELUCTANT VOLUNTEER
Taking to heart the notion 'Why have a dog and bark yourself?', Sir George Cayley volunteered his understandably reluctant coachman to make the first manned flight. On a still day in 1853 the glider made a short 55-yard (50m) hop across Brompton Dale. The coachman, relieved to have survived unscathed, but unwilling to entertain thoughts of another death-defying flight, resigned on the spot.

Peaceful Brompton has another claim to historic fame – poet William Wordsworth married a local lass, Mary Hutchinson, here in 1802

GOATHLAND'S SHEEP

The hardy sheep wander straight off the moortops to graze Goathland's wide green verges, and they roam the village with a distinctly proprietorial air. Curb your speed as you drive through, as the sheep reckon they have precedence over cars. They are so tame and accustomed to visitors that they will come right up to cars and picnickers in search of tasty morsels. Resist the temptation to offer them food, however, for it is unlikely to be suitable. The village bus shelters have gates to prevent sheep entering and leaving droppings!

AN UNUSUAL INN SIGN

How many pubs can boast an inn sign painted by a member of the Royal Academy? The sign over the door at the Birch Hall Inn at Beck Hole near Goathland is an oil painting by Sir Algernon Newton RA, father of Robert Newton, the rather more famous actor.

GOATHLAND   Map ref NZ8301

This pleasant village has achieved fame by proxy as the location for the popular television series, *Heartbeat*. On the small screen Goathland is transformed into Aidensfield, where PC Mike Bradley (the actor Jason Durr) treads his rural beat. Episodes are filmed throughout the moors, but the village of Goathland will be especially familiar to viewers; there is no need to search for locations the cameras have blessed.

Goathland was a popular destination for visitors long before the television series began, and though by no means the prettiest village on the moors, it is certainly well worth visiting in its own right. The broad grass verges, closely cropped by sheep, lead directly on to the heather and bracken of the moors. The village also makes an excellent centre for exploring the surrounding moorland and the stretch of Roman road known as Wade's Causeway (see page 92). Fame brings its own problems, however, and Goathland does get very busy on Bank Holidays.

The village's name is a little misleading. Black-faced moorland sheep are everywhere, local farmers enjoy grazing rights throughout the village, so the sheep roam where they will. They keep the grass closely cropped, but have only the most rudimentary road sense. However, you will look in vain for the goats of Goathland, because the village's name probably derives from the word 'gaut', meaning a gorge or water channel. These landscape

Beck Hole, a short stroll from the station at Goathland, is popular with walkers on the route of the North Yorkshire Moors preserved railway

features were created by the action of meltwater after the last Ice Age, and a brief investigation of the village and its surroundings will reveal a number of delightful waterfalls. The best-known is the 70-foot (21-m) Mallyan Spout, easily reached via a footpath adjacent to the Mallyan Spout Hotel.

The hotel's Victorian architecture is both a contrast to the traditional design of moorland buildings and a reminder that the first influx of visitors came with the building of the railway in the 1830s. Before that, the village's moorland setting kept it in relative isolation. Goathland's church, just a century old, but on a site of Christian worship for a thousand years, was furnished by Robert Thompson of Kilburn. Look for the little carved mice that were the craftsman's trademark. Near the church is a pinfold, a small, square paddock enclosed by stone walls, where stray beasts could be temporarily corralled until claimed by their owners.

Goathland was one of the stations on the main Whitby–Pickering line, a status it retains now that the once-defunct line has a new lease of life as the North Yorkshire Moors Railway. The steepest section of the line was known as the Beck Hole Incline, so steep that the earliest carriages had to be hauled up and down by using a system of counter-balanced weights: a hazardous procedure. Though tiny and unspoilt today, Beck Hole was briefly, during the middle of the last century, a busy centre of ironstone mining.

Houses of the village are well spaced around a rough, sheep-cropped green

THE COLOURFUL MOORS

Leave Goathland in any direction and you soon find yourself on expansive heather moorland. Though blackened in winter (hence the old name for the moors: 'Blackamore') the heather bursts into life during July, August and September, when mile after mile of tiny flowers paint the uplands purple. The bell heather has flowers of deep purple, while those of the cross-leaved heather have a pinker hue. The scene is made even more colourful during late summer by the blue-black bilberries and the rich browns of the bracken.

Hackness and the River Derwent

Just inland from the bright lights of Scarborough, this walk takes in the banks of the River Derwent, from the wooded Forge Valley past the secluded village of Hackness.

Time: 3 hours. Distance: 5½ miles (8.6km).
Location: 4½ miles (7.2km) northwest of Scarborough.
Start: The Forge Valley is well supplied with parking bays along the road going north from East and West Ayton. Park at the one named Old Man's Mouth.
(OS grid ref: SE984871.)
OS Map: Outdoor Leisure 27 (North York Moors – Eastern area) 1:25,000.
See Key to Walks on page 123.

ROUTE DIRECTIONS

Cross the nearby footbridge over the infant River Derwent and bear right to follow the river on raised duckboards. Your path continues through low-lying pasture. The weir on your right marks the beginning of a **sea cut**, designed to divert floodwaters to the sea. From here to Cockrah House the path is easy to follow, as it doesn't stray far from the river.

As you approach Cockrah House skirt the farmyard to the left. Go right along the farm road, then right again by cottages. Immediately before a bridge over the river, take a footpath to the left and follow the river to a footbridge. At the main road turn left and almost immediately take a path on the right uphill and turn left to skirt Greengate Wood. As **Hackness Hall** and its lake come into view the path turns to run just inside the wood.

Once past the hall, turn right on to a road and continue to shortly take a path to the right, opposite a ford over Crossdales Beck. Skirt the edge of Greengate Wood to cross a stile and continue uphill through the woods. A broad track narrows to a path between steep banks, before emerging at the top of the wood into open farmland. Join an unmade track to the right; it soon becomes a metalled road.

A leafy footpath leads beside the River Derwent, in the Forge Valley

The Sea Cut

The Derwent meanders along the flat valley floor; in days gone by the river used to flood farmland for miles around. Scalby Cut was the brainchild of Sir George Cayley of Brompton in the early 19th century. He was an enterprising man, better known as a pioneer of flight. Sir George saw that the damage to farmland could be prevented by diverting floodwater into the North Sea near Scarborough, and this channel was his successful response.

Hackness Hall

Hackness Hall, the 18th-century seat of Lord Derwent and not open to the public, enjoys an enviable position, surrounded by deeply cut, wooded valleys. The site of the Hall was once occupied by a nunnery, founded in AD 680 by St Hilda, Abbess of Whitby Abbey. The small lake near the Hall is probably the community's original fishpond.

The Forge Valley

The steep-sided Forge Valley was cut at the end of the last Ice Age, though the name itself dates back only as far as the 14th century when iron forges, thought to have been worked by the monks of Rievaulx Abbey, were fuelled by timber felled from this ancient woodland. Today the Forge Valley is known as a beauty spot and is popular with both walkers and bird-watchers. In summer these woods come alive with bird-song, and the native deciduous trees form a pleasing contrast to the conifer forests.

When it bears left, your route is straight ahead, down a track signed 'Suffield Ings Farm'.

A diverted path takes you left of the farm buildings. There is a dramatic panorama of Scarborough and its castle to the left. The path then drops downhill into Hawthorn Wood. Enjoy further panoramic views towards the **Forge Valley** as you emerge from the woods and go through a gate. The path soon bears left towards the right-hand end of a wood. Go through a gate and walk downhill on a farm track, fringed by a windbreak of ancient hawthorn trees. Go to the right of the farmyard of Mowthorpe Farm and walk left along the road. Within a few yards cross the sea cut. Keep on the road, back to the steep wooded slopes of the Forge Valley and the start point of the walk.

THE GHOST OF HACKNESS
The ghost of Hackness was the inspired invention of an 18th-century vicar's daughter when she found herself short of spending money. She reported seeing a spectral figure who intimated that a sum of £50 would allow his soul to be put at rest!

HACKNESS Map ref SE9790

Steep-sided, wooded valleys fan out from the lovely village of Hackness, established at the point where Lowdale Beck meets the River Derwent. It's hard to believe that this secluded spot is only 3 miles (4.8km) from the outskirts of Scarborough. St Hilda, Abbess of Whitby Abbey, established a nunnery here in AD 680, with Abbess Œdilburga; two centuries later Danish invaders razed it to the ground. The community rose from the ashes in the 11th century, finally to disappear in 1539 on the orders of Henry VIII.

Hackness Hall (not open to the public), a handsome Georgian house built in 1791 by lord of the manor Sir John Vanden Bempole Johnstone, occupies the site where the nunnery once stood. The only major evidence of that community is the lake, which may have served as a fishery. A more tangible relic, a fragment of an Anglo-Saxon cross, is displayed inside St Peter's Church. Inscriptions, in English, Latin and runic characters, offer up praise to Abbess Œdilburga and prayers for the nuns' own safety. When the cross was carved, possibly in the 9th century, the nuns may have been aware of the cruel fate that awaited them at the hands of marauding Danes.

While Hackness hides in its valley, you can enjoy panoramic views by taking the minor roads to the hilltop villages of Broxa and Silpho. Immediately to the south of Hackness is the Forge Valley, a beautiful, wooded dale created at the end of the Ice Age by glacial

The ancient foundations of St Peter's at Hackness were laid during the 11th century

meltwater. The River Derwent was diverted from its original direct route, east to the sea at Scalby, to flow south into the Humber.

The beautiful Forge Valley, which takes its name from the ironworks established here by the monks of Rievaulx Abbey, is a haven for wildlife. The woods on either side of the river feature native species, including oak, ash, elm and willow, as a pleasant contrast to the regimented conifer plantations which blight rather too many hillsides. Woodpeckers drum insistently; wagtails search for food along the riverbank; tiny warblers fill the woods with song each summer.

The walking is excellent at any season of the year; our Walk on page 100 is just one of many possible routes. The popularity of the Forge Valley is emphasised by the provision of car parks and picnic sites. Follow the road south through the woods to emerge at the villages of West and East Ayton, astride both the River Derwent and the main A170. At this point the Derwent is a mere 4 miles (6.4km) from Scarborough, yet it still has many miles to flow before it reaches the seat at the mouth of the Humber. The river bridge was constructed in 1775, from stone salvaged from the 14th-century castle that once stood near by. Built as a pele tower, a design more common further north, Ayton Castle survives as a ruin.

HOLE OF HORCUM Map ref SE8594

This remarkable landform, sometimes known as the Devil's Punchbowl, is a huge natural amphitheatre seemingly scooped out of Levisham Moor. Motorists on the A169 Pickering–Whitby road skirt the rim of the Hole of Horcum, and so many stop to gaze in wonderment, and follow some of the good paths in the area, that a large car park has been provided.

SALT
Since Anglo-Saxon times salt had been valued for its use in curing meat and fish; it was so valuable that a special tax was levied on it. The River Tees, to the north of the National Park, was the site of important salt pans. Tidal waters were evaporated to leave their salt solution, and salt roads – known as saltersgates – led towards Rievaulx, Old Byland and other monastic communities in the north.

Burning back the heather in the Hole of Horcum is all part of land management, allowing fresh new shoots to grow

The Hole of Horcum, a vast natural amphitheatre, offers good opportunities for walks

A SMUGGLERS' TALE

The smuggling of untaxed salt led to a tragedy. An excise man arrived incognito at the Saltersgate Inn, hoping to catch the smugglers 'red-handed'. When his motives were discovered he was murdered and his body concealed behind the fireplace. From that day, almost 200 years ago, the turf fire has never been allowed to go out. It's a nice story; you can still sit by the fire today and decide for yourself whether it's true. Or you can just take it with a pinch of salt...

Many stories account for the origin of the Hole of Horcum; take your pick between the factual and the fanciful. Legend tells that Wade, a local giant, scooped up a handful of earth to throw at his wife, Bell, thus creating the huge landform. Apparently, he missed her and the clod of earth landed to form Blakey Topping, little more than a mile (1.6km) away. To judge from the plethora of folk tales, Wade and his wife spent much of their time tossing missiles at one another. But the origin of the Hole of Horcum is rather more prosaic, scoured over millennia by glacial meltwater.

Just beyond a steep hairpin bend is the Saltersgate Inn, one of the many solitary inns in the National Park. They were generally sited on junctions of well-used tracks, catering for people on the move, as, indeed, they still do today. But instead of holiday-makers, those who stood at the bar of the Saltersgate Inn were more likely to have been hauliers leading trains of laden packhorses across the moors. Later it catered for stagecoach traffic, and was the site of a tollbooth when the road became a turnpike.

Saltersgate Inn, which lies on an old salt road linking the port of Whitby with the market town of Pickering, is regularly cut off by snow. Photographs displayed in the bar show the pub almost buried beneath drifts. In less inclement weather it's a convenient port of call after walking around the Hole of Horcum.

LEVISHAM AND LOCKTON Map ref SE8390/SE8489
Levisham and Lockton are a pair of delectable villages lying off the A169, about 5 miles (8km) north of Pickering. Lockton merited an entry in the Domesday Book, as Loca's Farm. Until 1938 the most prominent feature of the typically squat stone church was an ash tree growing out of the top of the square tower. It was removed and replanted in the churchyard, but it failed to thrive. Apart from that, the village has a youth hostel, a duck pond (sadly, few other village ponds in the National Park have survived intact) and limestone cottages set back from wide grass verges.

Neighbouring Levisham is a mere mile (1.6km) away, but it is a long mile if you happen to be on foot, for the villages are divided by a deep gorge. At the bottom, near Levisham Beck, is a converted watermill and the ruins of St Mary's Church. Though it was built in this isolated spot to be equidistant from both villages, it can hardly be said to be convenient for either.

Levisham, too, appears in the Domesday Book – as Leofgeat's homestead. Houses, and the Horseshoe Inn, surround an extensive village green. Pass the pub to join a single track road, with lovely long views along well-wooded Newton Dale. Continue down the road to arrive at Levisham Station, one of the stops for steam trains on the preserved line between Grosmont and Pickering. The public road ends at a level crossing; to continue on the forest drive at the far side of the line you must pay a toll.

LEVISHAM MOOR

Levisham Moor is one of the earliest sites where iron-smelting remains have been discovered. The finding of an Iron-Age smelting furnace indicates that iron tools were being made here before the Romans had arrived. Traces of ancient earthworks can be found on the moors immediately to the north of Levisham.

Good paths lead away from both Levisham and Lockton on to Levisham Moor, and beyond – to the Hole of Horcum. Since most people start from the car park on the A169, this is a good way to avoid the crowds.

The pretty moorland village of Levisham looks out over Newton Dale

THE BECK HOLE INCLINE

The section of the original line of the North Yorkshire Railway between Beck Hole and Goathland (bypassed in 1865) consisted of a 1-in-10 incline. Coaches had to be winched up and down with an imaginative arrangement of counter-balanced weights. Primitive though it was, the moorland railway was immediately hailed as a wonder of engineering.

Steam trains haul their passengers nostalgically through some of the finest scenery of the North York Moors during the summer

THE NORTH YORKSHIRE MOORS RAILWAY

The North Yorkshire Moors Railway has been a remarkable success story. No visit to the moors would be complete without a trip along this most scenic of lines.

Today the line is purely recreational, but it was commerce and industry that provided the original spur for the line to be built. Two centuries ago Whitby was one of the most important ports in the country. By the early 1800s, however, the town's traditional industries – whaling, ship building and alum mining – were in decline and Whitby's traders decided that the town needed better communications over land.

In 1831, George Stephenson, fresh from his engineering triumphs on the Stockton and Darlington Railway, surveyed the terrain between Whitby and Pickering, and with the limited budget at his disposal he recommended a railway line on which the carriages would be horse-drawn.

A veritable army of navvies was hired in 1833 to drive the line across the moors. Armed only with pick and shovel they tackled the rough terrain. The line from Whitby to Pickering was opened, with the usual fanfare, in 1836, when a train-load of dignitaries was pulled along the track at a sedate 10 miles per hour.

The line had the anticipated effect of revitalising the area; a variety of industries, such as ironstone mining, sprang up once a regular train service had been established. A few years later it was converted to carry steam trains; the first one chugged into Whitby in 1847. The troublesome Beck Hole Incline was bypassed, by blasting a new route between Beck Hole and Goathland. By the time a new century dawned the moors and coast were well served with rail links; the trains not only

transported goods, they also began to bring visitors from the crowded cities to enjoy the moorland landscape.

In 1965, as a result of the Beeching Reports, nearly 130 years of rail services came to a halt. The Esk Valley line was reprieved, but the section of line between Pickering and Grosmont was unceremoniously closed. Eight years later, after much hard work, the line was reopened by the North Yorkshire Moors Railway Preservation Society. More than just another line run by enthusiasts, the North Yorkshire Moors Railway operates a full timetable from March to October.

The 18-mile (29-km) rail journey takes visitors into the heart of the moors. Today more than 300,000 passenger journeys are taken every year, making the railway the biggest single attraction within the National Park. Many travellers take the train from Pickering Station, which dates from 1845 and the advent of steam-hauled trains. Railway buffs will be happy to know that, a century and a half later, the age of steam hasn't completely disappeared. The line climbs into the spectacular, steep-sided, wooded gorge of Newton Dale, before arriving at Levisham Station. Trains also call at Newtondale Halt, the starting point for a number of waymarked walks.

The next stop is Goathland, a favourite destination for visitors, whether travelling by car or rail. With its waterfalls, Rail Trail and delightful moorland setting, the village is well worth exploring. The northern terminus of the North Yorkshire Moors Railway is Grosmont, where travellers can join the main Northern Spirit line between Middlesbrough and Whitby.

Goathland offers the prettiest of the five stations on the route, complete with gas-lamps and gardens

DETERMINED ENTHUSIASTS
After Beeching closed the line between Pickering and Grosmont in 1965, the story might have ended there, except that a body of railway enthusiasts, convinced that the line still had a viable future, formed themselves into the North Yorkshire Moors Railway Preservation Society. They managed to raise enough money to buy the trackbed from British Rail; then they restored the line and the stations along it. After much hard work from them, and other interested bodies, the line was partially reopened in 1969 and from end to end in 1973.

Fine views may be enjoyed from the heights of Pickering Castle

MEDIEVAL FRESCOES

The wall paintings in Pickering's church have had a chequered history. They were probably first hidden from view during a bout of puritanical zeal after the Reformation, when such images were considered idolatrous. Rediscovered in 1851, they were almost immediately concealed once again beneath layers of whitewash on the directions of a vicar who shared this puritanical outlook. Fortunately, the frescoes were revealed once again in 1878, and are now recognised as some of the best medieval church paintings in the country.

PICKERING Map ref SE7984

The market town of Pickering lies just to the south of the National Park. Overlooking the market place (markets each Monday) is the large parish church dedicated to Saints Peter and Paul. Hemmed in by houses and shops, the building is approached by gates (streets) and ginnels (alleys). Inside are some fine 15th-century frescoes, illustrating scenes from the lives of saints and martyrs. St George slays a dragon; Thomas à Becket expires in the cathedral; St Edmund raises his eyes towards heaven as arrows fired by Vikings pierce his flesh.

After the Norman Conquest, King William created outposts in the north to establish order and quell uprisings; Pickering was one of these strategic sites. The first castle was built to a basic motte and bailey design; by the 12th century the wooden keep and outer palisade had been rebuilt in stone. It was besieged by Robert the Bruce on one of his incursions south of the border. When the Scots inflicted a heavy defeat on the army led by Edward II in 1322, the king found shelter here.

The castle witnessed no further military action, and was used by a succession of monarchs as a hunting lodge. Some parts of the old forest are still royal properties, but Pickering Castle is now in the hands of English Heritage.

Beck Isle Museum, housed in a fine Regency building close to Pickering Beck, offers fascinating glimpses into the more recent past. Successive rooms are devoted to different aspects of bygone life in town and country; you can visit the cobblers, gents' outfitters, kitchen, barber's shop and even the bar of a public house. Outbuildings house a blacksmith's forge, wheelwright and a collection of old farming implements.

RAVENSCAR Map ref NZ9801

Great things were planned for Ravenscar. A developer called John Septimus Bland decided to build a holiday resort that he thought would rival Whitby and Scarborough. A station was built, Bland laid out the town's network of roads, put in a drainage system and began to build shops and houses. Plots of land were put up for sale. But that is as close as Ravenscar got to being a major resort. Bland's company went bankrupt, and construction work stopped. Despite the panoramic sea views, this exposed site was clearly unsuitable for such a major development. It is geologically unstable, and visitors would have been faced with an awkward descent to the stony beach far below.

You can still see Ravenscar's street layout today, though grass is growing where the buildings ought to have been. When the Raven Hall Hotel was built in 1774, it was simply Raven Hall. George III came here to recuperate from his bouts of madness and melancholia. The hotel was to have been the centrepiece of the resort; now it stands alone, its distinctive mock battlements a landmark for miles around.

The Romans built a signal station here; its foundations and an inscribed stone (on display in Whitby's Pannett Park Museum) were found when Raven Hall's own foundations were being laid. The signal station relayed warnings of Anglo-Saxon invaders to military bases.

This part of the coastline (in the care of the National Trust, visit their Coastal Centre in Ravenscar) was exploited as early as the 17th century for alum, a chemical used in dyeing to fix colours permanently. Remains of both the quarries and buildings (see Walk on page 110) can be found near Ravenscar.

RAVENSCAR'S COASTLINE

The fault-line that runs along the coast between Boulby and Scarborough is most clearly visible at Ravenscar. At low tide the rocky shoreline is revealed as a series of concentric curves; they are formed from alternating layers of hard and soft rock, eroded by the waves over millions of years.

This is also excellent walking country, on either the beach or cliff-top. The Walk on page 110 uses a section of the Cleveland Way, with a return along the trackbed of the old Whitby–Scarborough railway. Ravenscar also provides the finish to the 42-mile (67.2-km) hike, across the moors from Osmotherley, known as the Lyke Wake Walk.

The steep cliffs around Ravenscar have defied major development over the centuries, leaving clear views out to sea

Seascapes from Ravenscar

The outward walk is on a bracing clifftop path from Ravenscar, the resort that was never built. Easy walking on the way back, along an old railway trackbed. There are fine views all the way.

Time: 4 hours. Distance: 7 miles (11.3km).
Location: 7½ miles (12.1km) south of Whitby.
Start: There is easy parking on the road close to the National Trust Coastal Centre in Ravenscar.
(OS grid reference NZ981016.)
OS Map: Outdoor Leisure 27 (North York Moors – Eastern area) 1:25,000.
See Key to Walks on page 123.

ROUTE DIRECTIONS

In **Ravenscar** walk down the path that passes the **Coastal Centre**; soon you can see Robin Hood's Bay in the distance. The first part of this walk follows the Cleveland Way – look out for the waymarked signs. At the fork of tracks, keep right and descend to join a wider track. Soon you will see signs for the **Peak Alum Quarries**. The remains of this once-valuable industry are now owned by the National Trust.

The track soon levels out. Follow the sign 'Cleveland Way' at a stile, to walk along the cliff-top; cross a couple of footbridges and pass a World War II concrete 'pillbox'. As you approach Stoupebrow Cottage Farm, go through a stone stile and turn right on to a metalled road. Walk to the right, past Stoupe Bank Farm, as the road becomes a path leading steeply downhill to cross Stoupe Beck on a footbridge. Immediately over the beck take the path to the left, climbing steeply uphill; you leave the Cleveland Way here. Before the top of the hill, take a set of steps to the

right into a field. Walk alongside a hedge towards two farms ahead. Soon the path becomes a farm track between hedges.

At a minor crossroads continue ahead, between South House Farm on the left and Mill Beck Farm on the right. Pass through a gate and the track descends steeply to cross Mill Beck on a footbridge. Continue ahead, uphill, and over a stile, to a metalled road. Note the causeway stones on the right. These were laid to enable packhorses to go dryshod through the mire. Turn right, still uphill, and at the top by a gate and bench, take a waymarked path to the left, next to another gate. Follow the field edge, and soon bear left, downhill (aim for a solitary electricity pole) to join a track leading to a footbridge over a beck. The path then climbs uphill, between hedgerows, with more causeway stones underfoot.

At the top, bear right along a farm track through two gates to a bridge over a disused railway line. Cross the bridge and the stile

immediately on the left, then clamber down the bank on to the trackbed. The railway line was opened in 1885 and was one of the country's most scenic lines until it was axed in 1965 by Dr Beeching. It is now a permissive path.

Walk along the trackbed to the right. From here it is good walking, slightly rising, almost back to your car. You soon reach the white-painted Fylinghall Stationmaster's House, and can pass either side of the station platform just beyond. Take the steps down, cross the road, and go up more steps to rejoin the trackbed.

As you approach Browside Farm, extensive views open up of farmland with Robin Hood's Bay beyond. Soon the view is of Ravenscar and particularly the Raven Hall Hotel perched high on the cliff-top. Further traces of the alum mining industry can be seen towards the end of the

The Cleveland Way passes by Ravenscar

some of the proposed street layouts are all that remain of 19th-century plans to turn Ravenscar into a holiday resort to rival nearby Whitby. The headland offers extensive views – an aspect appreciated by the Romans, who built one of their signal stations here (see page 109).

Coastal Centre

The National Trust's Coastal Centre at Ravenscar, open from April to October, has exhibits about North Yorkshire's Heritage Coast, showing why this stretch of coastline needs to be preserved. A marine aquarium provides an insight into the teeming life to be found in rockpools.

Peak Alum Quarries

Many parts of what is now the National Park were mined for alum, and here just north of Ravenscar are the remains of some industrial buildings which are now in the care of the National Trust.

walk. Leave the railway trackbed where it goes into a tunnel and continue uphill and back into Ravenscar and your car.

POINTS OF INTEREST

Ravenscar

The Raven Hall Hotel, a scattering of houses and

THE ST IVES OF THE NORTH

A number of artists have settled in Robin Hood's Bay, making the village almost the St Ives of the north. Many of the tales about Robin Hood's Bay have come from the pen of novelist Leo Walmsley, who recreated the village in his books, including *Three Fevers*, as 'Bramblewick'. He lived here from 1894 until 1913, and his stories of hardy fishing folk were very popular between the wars. Recently reprinted, Walmsley's books may yet find a new readership.

ROBIN HOOD

The fabled archer, wearer of Lincoln green and scourge of the rich, is a difficult character to pin down. Despite his links with Sherwood Forest, there are many sites in Yorkshire – including Wakefield and Scarborough – that claim Robin Hood as 'one of their own'. But, ironically, this little fishing village is the only one that actually bears his name.

CYCLING

The old railway line from Robin Hood's Bay to Ravenscar (5 miles/8km) is ideal for cycling. If you want to cycle downhill start from the Ravenscar end.

ROBIN HOOD'S BAY   Map ref NZ9505

Robin Hood's Bay vies with Staithes for the title of the prettiest fishing village on Yorkshire's coastline. Both communities have to juggle the conflicting demands of tourism with the needs of local people. To visit Robin Hood's Bay – or just 'Bay', as it's known locally – be sure to leave your car at the top of the hill where there are two large car parks. The road down to the beach is a cul-de-sac and visitors' cars are barred.

In any case the village has to be explored on foot. Apart from the access road, the houses – which cling precariously to the side of the cliff – are reached by narrow alleyways and steps. The result is architectural anarchy, a charming jumble of whitewashed cottages and red-tiled roofs leading down the main street and almost into the sea. An old story exaggerates only slightly when telling of a ship which at high tide came so close to shore that its bowsprit knocked out the window of a pub!

There is no harbour. Where once there were more than a hundred fishing boats, there are now just a handful, and they are launched down a slipway. Many of the old fishermen's cottages are now holiday homes. There is a good stretch of sandy beach and a rocky foreshore; children love to investigate the little rock pools left in these scars by the receding tide. Take care, it is notoriously easy to get cut off by the tide when it starts coming in again.

Robin Hood's Bay has had its share of storms, their effects exacerbated by the softness of the rock that forms the cliffs. In 1780 the main street was washed away, and over the years many houses in the village have been lost to the ravages of high winds and heavy seas. Today, a sea wall helps to blunt the worst of the buffeting, though every winter still brings memorable storms.

The only community of any size between Whitby and Scarborough, the relative isolation of Robin Hood's Bay helped to make it a haunt of smugglers. It used to be said that a boat-load of contraband could be beached, and the load transferred to the top of the village through a maze of secret passages between the tightly packed houses, all without seeing the light of day. It's not hard to imagine smugglers landing their booty here, and manhandling kegs and chests along the narrow alleyways.

No one knows why this fishing village should bear the name of Robin Hood, though there are as many theories as there are weeks in the year. One story tells that the outlaw was chased to the coast, and only evaded capture by disguising himself as a fisherman. According to another story he fired his bow from Whitby Abbey and the arrows landed here – 5 miles (8km) away!

You can walk at low tide along the beach (keep an eye out for the incoming tide) to Ravenscar, high on its cliff-top to the south, or take the Walk on page 110 along a

fascinating section of the Cleveland Way. On your way, about a mile (1.6km) from Robin Hood's Bay, is Boggle Hole, a little wooded cove. An old water mill, once powered by Mill Beck, is now a youth hostel conveniently situated for Cleveland Wayfarers.

The ever-popular village of Robin Hood's Bay appears to tip straight down the hillside

The Charming Village of Thornton-le-Dale

A walk through woods and fields from one of Yorkshire's 'picture postcard' villages, passing an evocative little Anglo-Saxon church in the hamlet of Ellerburn. Parts of the woodland track may be muddy in wet weather.

Time: 2½ hours. Distance: 5½ miles (8.9km).
Location: 2½ miles (4km) east of Pickering.
Start: Leave your car in the village car park, or one of the many parking bays near by. (OS grid reference SE836831.)
OS Map: Outdoor Leisure 27 (North York Moors – Eastern area) 1:25,000.
See Key to Walks on page 123.

ROUTE DIRECTIONS

Leave **Thornton-le-Dale** on the A170 in the direction of Pickering. Towards the top of a hill, a road branches off to the right. About 50 yards (46m) further on, look for a stile in a thick hedgerow, also to the right. A path takes you across fields and over stiles to reach a field with a pylon in it. Turn right along a stony track, and then turn left by a hedgerow and follow the path into Hagg Wood. A clear path leads downhill to Hagg House.

Cross a track and pass through a series of gates through a farm into a copse, where you join a track fringed with trees. The track sweeps to the right, downhill, to take you along the floor of the evocatively named Howl Dale. This shallow valley is well wooded, with conifers to the left and deciduous trees to the right. If the track is boggy, you can find a drier and a parallel alternative through the trees a few yards to your left.

Keep to this track, ignoring other paths that branch off, to enjoy the woodland walk. About 220 yards (201m) after the woodland ends on the left, the track swings to the right, steeply uphill. Once out of the woods the track levels off into fields. Follow the track along a hedgerow and soon bear left along a stone wall eventually meeting a more substantial farm track. Turn right; this track soon brings you on to a road.

Go left along the road for some way and turn right along another road, which is signposted 'Low Dalby Forest Drive'. When this road bends left, your route is sharply to the right, following a footpath sign downhill into woodland, before emerging through fields. The path soon brings you down to the tiny hamlet of Ellerburn and the

Pleasing cottages of golden Yorkshire stone are to be found in Thornton-le-Dale

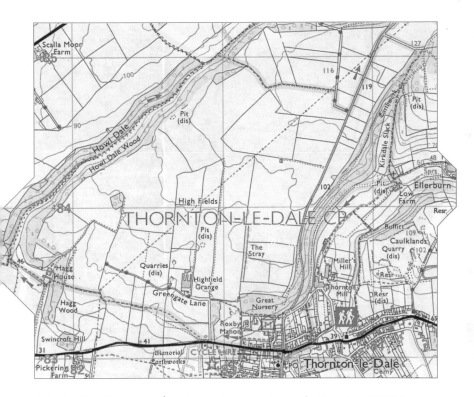

diminutive **Church of St Hilda**.

Immediately after the church, take a road to the right. Pass Ellerbeck Mill, and bear right when you reach another road. Look out, after a few yards, for a white gate and a footpath sign to your left; this brings you back into Thornton-le-Dale and the start of the walk.

POINTS OF INTEREST

Thornton-le-Dale
Thornton-le-Dale is one of North Yorkshire's 'honeypot' villages. Try to time your visit outside the busier holiday periods, for Thornton-le-Dale is best explored when the crowds are gone. The village green has a set of wooden stocks

and a slender, stepped market cross. Seventeenth-century almshouses are still used for their original purpose. Matthew Grimes, one of Napoleon's guards on the island of St Helena, is buried in the churchyard, 22 yards (20m) due east of the chancel.

Church of St Hilda
The tiny Church of St Hilda in Ellerburn can claim Anglo-Saxon origins and a number of eccentric vicars during its long history. The church has many examples of Viking stone work, including several cross heads and a serpent sculpture.

The tiny Church of St Hilda at Ellerburn

*The breezy queen of holiday
resorts, Scarborough has
retained both its popularity
and its dignity*

AN IMPREGNABLE FORTRESS
Scarborough Castle has never
been taken by force. When
the castle was besieged by the
Roundheads in 1645 a deep
well provided a good supply
of fresh water for the Royalist
inhabitants. However, the
beleaguered soldiers inside
the castle eventually ran out
of food, and were reduced to
eating rats and deriving what
little sustenance was available
by boiling up their leather
belts and boots.

SCARBOROUGH Map ref TA0488

The resort of Scarborough can claim to be one of the
oldest in the country. Its prosperity can be traced back to
the occasion, in the year 1620, when a visitor, Mrs
Elizabeth Farrow, was drinking a glass of spring water.
Finding the water acidic in taste, she came to the natural
conclusion that something so unpleasant must surely
have medicinal qualities too.

Promises of miraculous cures have always had willing
ears, the more outlandish the better. Scarborough's
spring water was said to cure many ills, even
hypochondria: surely a rather self-defeating exercise,
since hypochondriacs were precisely the sort of people to
whom the town extended the warmest welcome.
Scarborough's spring water certainly contains Epsom
salts and a cocktail of minerals. It was definitely good for
one thing – giving Scarborough's economy a much-
needed shot in the arm. The taking of the waters was
soon put on a more commercial footing. Scarborough
became known as a spa town; a name borrowed from the
Belgian resort. Scarborough was put firmly on the map as
a place where the well-heeled might come to recuperate
at leisure. Emboldened by this success, a local doctor
started to extol the health-giving properties of sea
bathing. One way or another Scarborough's waters were
responsible for its success.

The first spa house was built over the original spa well

in 1700. However, it was to suffer the fate shared by many other Scarborough buildings, by falling into the sea. Ever more elaborate spa houses were built, each one getting the royal stamp of approval for the water's efficacy. By the time Queen Victoria ascended to the throne, Scarborough was arguably the North's finest resort; many of the town's most distinguished buildings date from her reign. The Grand Hotel, overlooking the South Bay, seems to sum up the prosperity of Scarborough during the busiest time in its long history.

Scarborough Castle has dominated the town with an air of impregnability for the best part of a millennium. Standing proudly on its headland, between the North and South Bays, it enjoys an uninterrupted view over the town and out to sea. Remains of even earlier defences have been unearthed, including an Iron-Age settlement and a Roman signal station.

The Norman edifice we see today can be dated to the year 1136, when William de Gros decided to rebuild in stone an earlier wooden fort. Henry II, concerned that many nobles were growing too powerful, set about destroying their castles. He left Scarborough Castle alone, however. Impressed by its impregnability, he requisitioned the castle and kept it for himself.

Besieged on a number of occasions, Scarborough Castle was never taken by force, but only by starving the defenders into surrendering. On one occasion, in 1645, Hugh Chomley's Royalist troops were besieged by John Meldrum's Scottish army and the Great Keep was badly damaged by the Scottish artillery. Unable to hold out any longer, they were allowed to surrender with honour intact; those men who could still stand were allowed to march out of the castle. The castle was beseiged again in 1648 when the Parliamentary garrison, discontented

A MIRACULOUS CURE
Elaborate claims were made for the ailments which the spring waters at Scarborough might cure. Once stomach ache, consumption, rheumatism and fever had been taken care of, the waters would sort out palsy, madness and leprosy.

The impressive sweep of Scarborough's sandy South Bay

because they had not been paid, went over to the King's side; they too were starved into submission.

St Mary's Church also suffered artillery damage by the Royalists defending the castle; the damage is still visible. Anne Brontë was visiting Scarborough in 1849 when she succumbed to tuberculosis and died. The author of *The Tenant of Wildfell Hall* is buried in the churchyard.

While many of our resorts have lost out to the ease of foreign travel, Scarborough has enough attractions to keep the most fastidious visitors coming back for more. Cricket lovers eagerly anticipate the Scarborough Festival, traditionally held towards the end of the season. Playwright Alan Ayckbourn keeps faith with local theatre-goers by premiering most of his plays here before they are transferred to London's West End.

'FLINT JACK'

Sleights was the birthplace, in 1815, of 'Flint Jack', who delighted in fooling those experts who came to the moors in search of antiquities. He established a lucrative sideline by manufacturing his own relics, and offering them to collectors and museums as genuine archaeological finds. His fakes and forgeries were so convincing that even the British Museum was fooled into parting with money.

Enjoy the Esk Valley from the river at Sleights

SLEIGHTS Map ref NZ8607

Sleights straddles the River Esk in a sheltered dip in the landscape, just outside the boundary of the National Park. There are few buildings here to attract the eye, but it is a convenient spot from which to explore the surrounding countryside – whether you head for open moorland, or the more intimate environs of the Esk.

Ruswarp, between Sleights and the sea, marks the tidal limit of the River Esk. Here, on a quiet stretch of the river, you can hire a dinghy for a leisurely row, until you hear those immortal words: 'Come in number nine'.

A minor road from Sleights leads you to a hamlet that glories in the delicious name of Ugglebarnby. The meaning is 'the farm of old owl beard'; the explanation is less easy to fathom. Continue past Ugglebarnby to arrive in Littlebeck, on a road that snakes through this delightful village. Here you can enjoy fine walks, one along May Beck and the other to the south to see Falling Foss, an exquisite waterfall in a woodland setting.

THORNTON-LE-DALE   Map ref SE8383

Despite being split in two by the A170, Thornton-le-Dale is still one of the prettiest villages in Yorkshire. The thatched cottage beside Dalby Beck must be one of the most photographed buildings in the county, making regular appearances on calendars and biscuit tin lids. The boundary of the National Park makes a little detour to include the village; a good indication that it is worth taking the time to explore.

The tone is established by the beck; its meandering course through the village is punctuated by a succession of tiny bridges. At the crossroads, in the centre of the village, is a small green where the market cross and a set of stocks still stand. On the opposite side of the road are Lady Lumley's Almshouses, a block of twelve dwellings, built in 1670 and still retaining their original use.

The churchyard is the burial place of Matthew Grimes, who died in 1875 at the grand old age of 96. His claim to fame is that he guarded Napoleon during the emperor's exile on the island of St Helena, and helped to carry his body to the grave. Thornton-le-Dale's churchyard is also the last resting place of Sir Richard Chomley, known as The Great Black Knight of the North. He served at the court of Elizabeth I; his home, Roxby Castle, once stood just to the west of Thornton-le-Dale. His effigy can be seen inside the church.

The Walk on page 114 explores the countryside around the village and the Saxon church in the tiny hamlet of Ellerburn. To explore further afield take the Forest Drive (toll payable) through Dalby Forest, easily accessible by driving north from Thornton-le-Dale.

Picturesque buildings line the streets of Thornon-le-Dale

SUPERSTITIONS

Superstitions were rife in rural areas. Charms considered lucky included a horseshoe (or stone with a natural hole in it), hung from the door of the house. Picking up a pin, or other piece of metal, would prevent a witch from using it in her spells. The rowan tree was known as witchwood; carrying a cross made of rowan wood was a common way to guard against the 'evil eye'.

Of course, those who scoff at such unsophistication should examine their own habits: crossing the fingers, playing 'lucky' lottery numbers...

The Eastern Moors and the Coast

Leisure Information

Places of Interest

Shopping

The Performing Arts

Sports, Activities and the Outdoors

✓ **Checklist**

Annual Events and Customs

Leisure Information

TOURIST INFORMATION CENTRES
Pickering
The Ropery. Tel: 01751 473791.
Scarborough
Pavilion House, Valley Bridge Road. Tel: 01723 373333.
Harbourside, Sandside. Tel: 01723 341000.

OTHER INFORMATION
English Heritage (Yorkshire Region)
37 Tanner Row, York. Tel: 01904 601901.
Environment Agency
Rivers House, 21 Park Sq South, Leeds. Tel: 0113 2440191.
Forest Enterprise
Outgang Road, Pickering.
Tel: 01751 472771.
Moorsbus summer coach and minibus
Tel 01439 770657.
www.moorsbus.net
National Trust
Goddards, 27 Tadcaster Road, York. Tel: 01904 702021.
www.nationaltrust.org.uk
North York Moors National Park
The Old Vicarage, Bondgate, Helmsley. Tel: 01439 770657.
www.northyorkmoors-npa.gov.uk

Yorkshire Tourist Board
312 Tadcaster Road, York. Tel: 01904 707961. www.ytb.org.uk
Yorkshire Wildlife Trust
10 Toft Green, York. Tel: 01904 659570. www.yorkshire-wildlife-trust.org.uk

ORDNANCE SURVEY MAPS
Landranger 1:50,000. Sheets 94, 100, 101.

Places of Interest

There will be an admission charge at the following places of interest unless otherwise stated.
Beck Isle Museum
Bridge Street, Pickering. Tel: 01751 473653. Open Mar–Oct, daily.
Crescent Arts Workshop
The Crescent, Scarborough. Tel: 01723 351461. Open all year, most days. Free.
North Yorkshire Moors Railway
Pickering Station, Pickering. Tel: 01751 472508. Open Apr–Oct daily, some winter weekends.
The Old Coastguard Station.
Robin Hood's Bay. Tel: 01947 885900. Open daily in summer; off season, weekends only.
Pickering Castle
Tel: 01751 474989. Open Apr–Oct daily; winter Wed–Sun.

Robin Hood's Bay Museum
Chapel Street. Tel: 01947 880097. Open Jun & Sep pm only; Jul & Aug all day.
The Rotunda Museum
Vernon Road, Scarborough. Tel: 01723 374839. Open all year, most days.
Scarborough Art Gallery
The Crescent. Tel: 01723 374753. Open all year, most days.
Scarborough Castle
Tel: 01723 372451. Open Apr–Oct, daily; winter closed Mon & Tue.
The Scarborough Millennium
Harbourside. Tel: 01723 501000. Open Apr–Sep, daily.
Sea-life & Marine Sanctuary
Scalby Mills, Scarborough. Tel: 01723 376125. Open all year, daily.
Staintondale Shire Horse Farm
Tel: 01723 870458. Open Jun–Sep, Tue, Wed, Fri & Sun.
Woodend Natural History Museum
The Crescent, Scarborough. Tel: 01723 367326. Open all year, most days.
Wordsworth Gallery
Gallows Hill. Tel: 01723 863298. Open all year, Mon–Sat.

SPECIAL INTEREST FOR CHILDREN

The following places may be of interest to visitors with children. Unless otherwise stated, there will be an admission charge.

Kinderland
Burniston Road, North Bay, Scarborough. Tel: 01723 354555. Open Apr–Sep, daily.

Staintondale Shire Horse Farm
Tel: 01723 870458. Open Jun–Sep, Tue, Wed, Fri & Sun.

Shopping

Pickering
Open-air market, Mon.

LOCAL SPECIALITIES

Arts and Crafts
The Stained Glass Centre, Killerby Lane, Cayton, Scarborough. Tel: 01723 581236.
Thornton-le-Dale Arts and Crafts. Tel: 01751 477404.

Ceramics
Green Man Gallery, 8 Park Street, Pickering. Tel: 01751 472361.

Honey
The Honey Farm, East Ayton. Tel: 01723 864001.

Ice Cream
Beacon Farm, Beacon Way, Sneaton. Tel: 01947 605212.

Trout
Moorland Trout Farm, Pickering. Tel: 01751 473101.

The Performing Arts

Spa Entertainment Complex
Scarborough. Tel: 01723 376774.

Spa Theatre
South Bay, Scarborough. Tel: 01723 365068.

Sports, Activities and the Outdoors

ANGLING

Sea
Scarborough
Boats for hire at the harbour in South Bay.

Fly
Larner's Lake, Wood House Farm, Little Ayton. Tel: 01642

722309.
Pickering Trout Lake. Tel: 01751 474219.
Wykeham Trout Lakes. Tel: 01723 863148.
The Mere, Scarborough. Day tickets on site.

BEACHES

There are sandy beaches with easy access at Robin Hood's Bay and Scarborough (North Bay and South Bay).

CRICKET

Scarborough
North Marine Road. Tel: 01723 365625.

CYCLE HIRE

Goathland
Moortrek Cycle Hire, Brereton Lodge. Tel: 01947 896100.

Wykeham
Wykeham Cycle Hire, St Helens Caravan Park. Tel: 01723 073262.

GOLF COURSES

Kirkbymoorside
Kirkbymoorside Golf Club, Manor Vale. Tel: 01751 431525.

Scarborough
North Cliff Golf Club, North Cliff Avenue. Tel: 01723 360786.
South Cliff Golf Club, Deepdale Avenue. Tel: 01723 365150.

HORSE-RIDING

Robin Hood's Bay
Farsyde Stud and Riding Centre. Tel: 01947 880249.

Snainton
Snainton Riding Centre.

Striding out on a quiet lane near Robin Hood's Bay

Tel: 01723 859218.

Staintondale
Wellfield Trekking Centre. Tel: 01723 870182.

LONG-DISTANCE FOOTPATHS AND TRAILS

The Rail Trail
A 3½-mile (5.6-km) walk from Goathland to Grosmont following the track bed of George Stephenson's original railway line.

Annual Events and Customs

Littlebeck
Littlebeck Rose Queen Ceremony, early August.

Pickering
Jazz Festival, late July.
Traction Engine Rally, early August.
Agricultural Show, mid-August.

Robin Hood's Bay
Folk Festival, June.

Scalby
Scalby Faire, early June.

Scarborough
Scarborough Fayre, June.
Morris Dance Festival, mid-June.
International Music Festival, late June.
Scarborough Cricket Festival, end August/September.

Thornton-le-Dale
Thornton-le-Dale Show, mid-August.

Atlas and Map Symbols

THE NATIONAL GRID SYSTEM

The National Grid system covers Great Britain with an imaginary network of 100 kilometre grid squares. Each square is given a unique alphabetic reference as shown in the diagram. These squares are sub-divided into one hundred 10 kilometre squares, each numbered from 0 to 9 in an easterly (left to right) direction and northerly (upwards) direction from the bottom left corner. Each 10 km square is similarly sub-divided into one hundred 1 km squares.

Kilometres
North

				HP	
			HT	HU	
			HY	HZ	
NA	NB	NC	ND		
NF	NG	NH	NJ	NK	
NL	NM	NN	NO		
	NR	NS	NT	NU	
	NW	NX	NY	NZ	
		SC	SD	SE	TA
		SH	SJ	SK	TF	TG
	SM	SN	SO	SP	TL	TM
	SR	SS	ST	SU	TQ	TR
SV	SW	SX	SY	SZ	TV

0 100 200 300 400 500 600 700
False Origin of National Grid   Kilometres East

KEY TO ATLAS

MOTORWAY

M4	Motorway with number
Fleet	Motorway service area
Toll	Motorway junction with and without number
	Restricted motorway junctions
	Motorway and junction under construction

PRIMARY ROUTE

A3	Primary route single/dual carriageway
Grantham North	Primary route service area
BATH	Primary route destinations
	Roundabout
5	Distance in miles between symbols
	Narrow Primary route with passing places

A ROAD

A1123	Other A road single/dual carriageway
	Road tunnel
Toll	Toll
	Road under construction
	Roundabout

B ROAD

B2070	B road single/dual carriageway
	B road interchange junction
	B road roundabout with adjoining unclassified road
	Steep gradient
	Unclassified road single/dual carriageway
	Railway station and level crossing

KEY TO ATLAS

Abbey, cathedral or priory		-----	National trail
Aquarium		NT	National Trust property
Castle		NTS	National Trust for Scotland property
Cave			Nature reserve
Country park		★	Other place of interest
County cricket ground		P+R	Park and Ride location
Farm or animal centre			Picnic site
Forest drive			Steam centre
Garden			Ski slope natural
Golf course			Ski slope artifical
Historic house		i	Tourist Information Centre
Horse racing			Viewpoint
Motor racing			Visitor or heritage centre
Museum			Zoological or wildlife collection
AA telephone			Forest Park
Airport			Heritage coast
Heliport			National Park (England & Wales)
Windmill			National Scenic Area (Scotland)

KEY TO TOURS

Tour start point		Buckland Abbey	Highlighted point of interest
Direction of tour			
Optional detour			Featured tour

KEY TO WALKS

Scale 1:25,000, 2½inches to 1 mile, 4cm to 1 km

	Start of walk		Line of walk
	Direction of walk	⊪▷	Optional detour
		Buckland Abbey	Highlighted point of interest

ROADS AND PATHS

M1 or A6(M)	M1 or A6(M)	Motorway
A 31(T) or A35	A 31(T) or A35	Trunk or main road
B 3074	B 3074	Secondary road
A 35	A 35	Dual carriageway
		Road generally more than 4m wide
		Road generally less than 4m wide
		Other road, drive or track
		Path

Unfenced roads and tracks are shown by pecked lines

RAILWAYS

Multiple track	Standard gauge	Embankment
Single track		Tunnel
Narrow gauge		Road over; road under
Siding		Level crossing
Cutting		Station

PUBLIC RIGHTS OF WAY

Public rights of way may not be evident on the ground

Public paths { footpath / bridleway }	Byway open to all traffic
Permissive path	Road used as a public path
Permissive bridleway	Named path
	Pennine Way — National trail or recreational path

The representation on this map of any other road, track or path is no evidence of the existence of a right of way

RELIEF

50 / 285	Heights determined by	{ Ground survey / Air survey }

Contours are at 5 and 10 metres vertical interval

SYMBOLS

	Place of worship { with tower / with spire, minaret or dome / without such additions }	∘W, Spr	Well, Spring
			Gravel pit
▢	Building		Other pit or quarry
▢	Important building		Sand pit
. T; A; R	Telephone: public; AA; RAC		Refuse or slag heap
--▢----- pylon pole	Electricity transmission line		County Boundary (England & Wales)
△ △	Triangulation pillar		Water
⇔	Bus or coach station		
⚲ ⚲	Lighthouse; beacon		Sand; sand & shingle
⊹	Site of antiquity		National Park boundary
NT	National Trust always open		Mud
FC	Forestry Commission		

DANGER AREA
Firing and test ranges in the area
Danger!
Observe warning notices

VEGETATION

Limits of vegetation are defined by positioning of the symbols but may be delineated also by pecks or dots

♣ ♣	Coniferous trees	⌒ ⌒	Non-coniferous trees
○ ○	Orchard		Heath
Ho Ho	Coppice		Marsh, reeds, saltings.

TOURIST AND LEISURE INFORMATION

⚑	Camp site	PC	Public convenience
🛈	Information centre	P	Parking
i	Information centre (seasonal)	☀	Viewpoint
⚏	Caravan site	⊕	Mountain rescue post
⊽	Picnic site		

Index

North Yorkshire Moors Railway above Grosmont

Acknowledgements

The author would like to thank Jill Renney and Karl Gerhardsen at the North York Moors National Park for their invaluable assistance.

The Automobile Association would like to thank the following photographers and libraries for their assistance in the preparation of this book.

All pictures except those listed below are held in the Association's own library (AA PHOTO LIBRARY) and were taken by John Morrison with the exception of the cover and page 72 (P Baker) 45, 106, 107, 127 (J Mottershaw) 53, 62, 97, 102, 118 (R Newton).

THE MANSELL COLLECTION LTD 7b.